D0478577

holiday *Sweets*

holiday *Sweets*

written by

GEORGEANNE BRENNAN

conceived & produced by

JENNIFER BARRY DESIGN

photography by

RICHARD G. JUNG

SMITHMARK

Copyright © 1999 Jennifer Barry Design
Text copyright © 1999 Georgeanne Brennan
Photographs copyright © 1999 Richard G. Jung

All rights reserved. No part of this publication may be reproduced, stored in
a retrieval system, or transmitted by any means electronic, mechanical, photocopying, or
otherwise without first obtaining written permission of the copyright owner.

This edition published in 1999 by SMITHMARK Publishers, a division of
U.S. Media Holdings, Inc., 115 West 18th Street, New York, NY 10011.

SMITHMARK books are available for bulk purchase for sales promotion
and premium use. For details, write or call the manager of special sales, SMITHMARK Publishers,
115 West 18th Street, New York, NY 10011.

Conceived and Produced by Jennifer Barry Design, Sausalito, California
Layout Production: Kristen Wurz
Food Stylist: Basil Friedman
Prop Stylist: Carol Hacker / Tableprop, San Francisco
Craft and Floral Stylist: Sarah Dawson
Copy Editor: Carolyn Miller
Proofreading: Barbara King

Library of Congress Cataloging-in-Publication Data
Brennan, Georgeanne.
Holiday sweets : a collection of inspired recipes, gifts, and decorations / written by Georgeanne Brennan ;
conceived & produced by Jennifer Barry Design ; photography by Richard G. Jung.
p.   cm.
Includes index.
ISBN 0-7651-1663-4
1. Desserts.   2. Holiday Cookery.   3. Holiday decorations.   I. Title.
TX773.B754   1999
641.8'6--dc21   99-18271   CIP

Printed in Hong Kong

First printing 1999
10 9 8 7 6 5 4 3 2 1

Acknowledgments

Georgeanne Brennan would like to thank the following people:

My husband, Jim Schrupp, for his enthusiastic recipe sampling and careful editing.

Robert Wallace for being such a helpful and interested kitchen assistant and recipe tester.

Ethel Brennan for her advice on candy making and baking, and the many friends who

shared family recipes and traditions. Thanks also to Jennifer Barry for asking me to participate

in her Holiday series and allowing me to be part of yet another of her beautiful books,

Carolyn Miller for her diligent editing, Basil Friedman for his food styling,

and Richard Jung for his photographs.

Jennifer Barry Design and the photography and styling team would like

to thank and acknowledge the following individuals for their help on this book project:

Smithmark editor Gabrielle Pecarsky for her continuing support and enthusiasm

for the Holiday series, Leslie Barry for her beautiful original series design, Juliet Jung for

the extraordinary frosted ornament cookies, photography assistant Ivy for her endless

reserve of patience and energy, and Tom Johnson for production assistance. Special thanks

go to Vicky Kalish and Cecelia Michaelis for their support of this project.

Introduction

Holiday sweets, made either for home or for gifts, bring visions of warm, fragrant kitchens and of festive baking with family and friends who are preparing to load the holiday tables with an array of gingerbread people, fudge, peanut brittle, rich tortes, and chocolate cakes. Airy fluffs of angel food cake swirled with whipped cream, frothy mousses of chocolate and peppermint, glazed jewel-like petits fours, and deep-dish apple-quince pie all come proudly forth from the kitchen. Glistening candied apples, satisfyingly sticky popcorn balls, and brilliantly colored lollipops are made especially for children, although most adults will happily partake of them as well.

White and brown sugar, molasses, and honey to caramelize in pies and candies; rich, smooth chocolate for toppings and fudge; toasted walnuts, pecans, and hazelnuts for candy crunching, cakes, and ice cream; and seasonal fruits are the pantry specialties. Dried fruits, peppermints, and a bevy of aromatic spices from cinnamon to cardamom and ginger add the high notes of intense flavors.

One of the greatest pleasures of holiday sweet making is to prepare a favorite cookie, pie, or cake to give as a gift. Homemade treats are particularly treasured in the current era of prepackaged convenience, and something special, made at home with loving care, is as fine a gift as you can give. It is rewarding to do the cooking when you know it will be appreciated by the recipient, and it is fun to package sweets in a creative, decorative way.

Sweets can also be decorative on their own. Simple craft projects can produce such finery as a colorful tabletop tree made entirely of chocolate candies, a stenciled gingerbread gift box, colorful wreaths of holiday candy, or a candy acorn kissing ball.

Holiday Cookies

There are many, many types of cookies, and almost all are suitable for holiday baking. Bar cookies, drop cookies, and rolled and hand-shaped cookies are among the most popular and the easiest to make, and require no special equipment or techniques.

Bar Cookies

Bar cookies, such as Apricot-Pistachio Bars (page 46), are made by spreading batter into a pan and baking it. The cookies are shaped later when they are cut. Sizes may vary according to your wishes. For example, if you want to make a number of bite-sized cookies, simply cut the bars into 1-inch squares. For dessert-sized portions, cut into 2-1/2-inch squares. Depending on the recipe, bar cookies may be soft, chewy, or crunchy. To make cookies with clean and smooth edges, use a sharp knife for cutting and wipe the knife with a damp cloth after each cut.

9

Drop Cookies

Drop cookies are exceedingly easy to make, even for the novice, and are a good choice for children's participation. Drop cookies are shaped by dropping or pushing the dough off a spoon. As they bake, the butter melts, the lumpiness smoothes, and the ingredients blend together. The size of the cookies can be controlled by the size of the drop. For large, party-sized cookies, drop larger pieces of dough. For small, bite-sized cookies, simply use smaller bits of dough.

Rolled Cookies

Rolled cookies such as gingerbread and sugar cookies are a particular holiday favorite because they lend themselves to being iced and then further decorated with chocolate, colored, or silver sprinkles; colored sugar; tiny pieces of peppermint; and dried or candied fruits. They are usually cut out with cookie cutters into Christmas trees, candy canes, bells, snowmen, ornaments, menorahs, dreidels, or other holiday motifs. You can devise your own shapes by making patterns or templates, first drawing the shape on cardboard and then cutting it out. The cardboard shapes can be used as stencils on rolled dough to be cut out with a paring knife. Ordinary drinking glasses can be turned upside down to cut out rounds, which are good choices for ornament cookies.

It is easiest to ice cookies when they are a still a little warm from the oven, as this helps the icing to spread evenly and smoothly over the cookies. While the icing is still soft, add any decorations desired.

Holiday Candies

Although most of us will purchase our holiday candies, there are some homemade favorites that are relatively easy to make and yield impressive results. Candies cover a wide range, from soft, creamy fudge to hard, brittle candies like lollipops and toffee. Candy making is both a science and an art, and is less forgiving of errors in measurement and timing than most other sweets. Candy is essentially made by combining some form of sugar—white or brown sugar, honey, or molasses—to make a syrup, which is then cooked to the desired temperature to produce soft, chewy, or hard candies. For the novice and professional alike, a candy thermometer is indispensable.

When making candy, be completely prepared with all the necessary utensils and give it your complete attention, as a moment's woolgathering may well ruin the batch when the desired temperature is quickly exceeded.

Homemade candy makes a very special holiday gift and can be beautifully packaged in silver and gold boxes, or bags of clear cellophane, then tied with a festive ribbon. Craft and food shops and candy-making suppliers will have an ample selection of boxes, waxed papers, candy cups, and bags.

Cakes and Pies

The holidays are the time to pull out all the stops and make those glamorous, showy, richly wonderful cakes and pies that make everyone at the table oooh and aaah. Angel food cake, swathed with whipped cream and covered with coconut is a vision in white. A warm, ultra-chocolate cake, decorated with a stencil of confectioners' sugar, will satisfy even the greatest chocolate lover, while tiny, bite-sized fruitcakes, well soaked with rum, make an elegant end to a perfect holiday meal. Cheesecake is always a welcome guest at the holiday table, especially when dressed for the occasion with a sprinkle of toasted hazelnuts and a hazelnut crust.

When cakes suit your fancy, choose a serving plate or cake stand slightly larger than your cake, leaving room to ornament it with sprigs of greenery, a wreath of sugared fruits, or mint sprigs.

Fruits, nuts, and chocolate make the best of holiday pies, whether in combination with each other or alone. The Double-Pecan Tart (page 94) is a variation on the Southern classic, and a deep-dish pie of apples and quince is a sure bet to draw raves from your guests. A European-style torte with a rich, sugary crust will satisfy even the most jaded palate, as will a golden puff pastry tart filled with spiced apples and cranberries.

To decorate your pies, top them with whipped cream, chocolate curls, or mint sprigs on each individual plate, or liberally sprinkle the plate with confectioners' sugar. A pool of crème anglaise beneath the pie gives a fancy impression and tastes good as well.

Holiday Puddings, Ices, and Creams

Puddings are an indelible part of the English tradition. Steamed plum pudding is the most memorable one, and while it is made in dozens of styles, the plum (actually a prune, or dried plum) remains an important, if not essential, ingredient, along with a heady assortment of spices and other dried fruit. The pudding is typically steamed in a lidded mold, (although a heatproof bowl may also be used) and is then unmolded to serve.

Other puddings include the once-humble bread pudding, now enriched and elevated by luscious ingredients such as figs, brandy, apples, cherries, and whipped cream. It may be made of various kinds of breads, including sweet breads such as croissants or brioches, as well as everyday table breads. When served warm in individual ramekins or in large scoops, well garnished with ice cream or whipped cream, it makes a fine finish to a holiday meal.

Creams or custards based on eggs and cream have a smooth, velvety consistency, and when topped with burnt sugar, make a very fancy dessert. Mousses too are egg based, but without milk or cream. Instead, the egg yolks are beaten with sugar and a flavoring, such as chocolate, orange, or vanilla, then blended with egg whites that have been beaten separately into soft peaks. The result is a delicate and frothy pudding, light as a dandelion puff on the wind.

Holiday ices, such as eggnog or peppermint ice cream, tend to be festive signals of the season. If you are short on time, simply purchase ready-made ice cream. It can be served with complementary sauces, which will elevate the ordinary to the sublime. Try dried cherry sauce for hazelnut ice cream, or sandwich the ice cream between cream puffs to make the French profiteroles and top them with freshly sugared fruits, such as grapes or kumquats.

When it comes to holiday glamour, puddings, ices, and creams are all excellent candidates for your creativity. Individual servings can be garnished with bits of holiday sweets, such as chocolate shavings, crushed peppermint, toasted nuts, candied fruits, or sugared flowers and leaves.

cakes & puddings

2

Plum Pudding with Hard Sauce

PLUM PUDDING IS AN OLD ENGLISH FAVORITE THAT DATES BACK SEVERAL HUNDRED YEARS. ESSENTIALLY A SPICED, MOIST, DARK CAKE FLAVORED WITH RAISINS AND SOMETIMES OTHER FRUITS AS WELL, IT IS FREQUENTLY SPRINKLED WITH BRANDY OR RUM, THEN WRAPPED AND LEFT TO AGE, OR "RIPEN." IT IS REHEATED IN ITS MOLD TO SERVE AND IS USUALLY ACCOMPANIED BY A SAUCE. THE SECRET INGREDIENT IS THE SUET, WHICH LIGHTENS THE CAKE. ORDER SUET, THE LEAF FAT SURROUNDING THE KIDNEY, FROM A BUTCHER.

1/2 cup chopped dried figs

1/2 cup chopped prunes

1/2 cup chopped dried apricots

1/2 cup dried currants

1/2 cup raisins

1/4 cup brandy

1/4 cup water

1/2 cup milk

4 ounces suet

1 cup all-purpose flour

1 teaspoon baking powder

1/2 teaspoon salt

1-1/2 teaspoons ground nutmeg

1-1/2 teaspoons ground cinnamon

1/2 teaspoon ground ginger

1/2 cup firmly packed dark brown sugar

1 egg

1 cup fresh bread crumbs

2 teaspoons finely grated orange zest

2 teaspoons finely grated lemon zest

1/4 cup orange juice

1/4 cup chopped walnuts

1 to 1-1/2 tablespoons butter

HARD SAUCE

1 cup (2 sticks) butter, softened

3 cups confectioners' sugar

1 teaspoon vanilla extract

1 teaspoon freshly grated nutmeg

1/2 cup brandy for flaming

14

In a large saucepan, combine the figs, prunes, apricots, currants, raisins, brandy, water, and milk. Bring to a boil over medium-high heat, then reduce heat to low and simmer until the fruit is plumped and tender and the mixture has formed a rather thick, moist paste. Set aside to cool.

Grind the suet through the smallest setting of a meat grinder, or chop it finely. The particles should be very small. Work quickly and handle the suet as little as possible to keep it chilled.

In a medium bowl, combine the flour, baking powder, salt, nutmeg, cinnamon, and ginger and mix well. Add the suet and work with your fingers until the suet has formed small, flour-coated particles. Set aside.

In a large bowl, beat the brown sugar and egg together until thickened, about 1 minute. Beat in the bread crumbs, orange zest, lemon zest, and orange juice. Stir in the walnuts. Add the flour mixture to the egg mixture, then beat in the cooled fruit mixture. Mix well.

With the butter, heavily grease a 5-cup plum pudding mold and its lid. Spoon the batter into the mold, smoothing the top. Fasten the lid. Place a rack on the bottom of a large pot. Put the mold on the rack. Add enough boiling water to cover two-thirds of the mold. Over high heat, bring the water to boiling again, then reduce heat to low. The water should simmer, not boil. Cover the pot and steam for 2 hours, maintaining a simmer and adding more boiling water if needed.

Remove the mold from the pot and let cool for 20 minutes before unmolding. Let cool completely.

To store, wrap the pudding in plastic wrap, then in aluminum foil. Store in the refrigerator for up to 1 month. To serve, grease the mold with butter, unwrap the pudding, put it back into its mold, and fasten the lid. Set it on a rack in the bottom of a large pot and pour in boiling water to reach two-thirds of the way up the sides of the mold. Steam again, as above, for 1 hour. Let stand 20 minutes, then unmold onto a serving plate.

To make the hard sauce: In a medium bowl, combine the butter, confectioners' sugar, vanilla, and nutmeg and beat on high speed until light and fluffy. Continue to beat and add 1/4 cup of the brandy. When it is well blended, spread some of the sauce across the top of the pudding; it will melt down the side. In a saucepan, warm the remaining brandy just to lukewarm. Pour it over the plum pudding, then, with a long-handled match, set it alight.

Cut the pudding into 1/2-inch-thick slices to serve, accompanied by the remaining hard sauce. *Serves 8*

Individual Apple Puddings with Crème Chantilly

THE FLOUR ELEMENT IN THIS CAKELIKE PUDDING IS BREAD, TORN INTO VERY SMALL PIECES, THEN FLAVORED WITH APPLE CIDER AND COINTREAU. WHEN UNMOLDED AND SERVED WARM, WITH A CREAM TOPPING, IT IS AN ELEGANT LIGHT DESSERT.

5 tablespoons butter

1/2 cup golden raisins

2 tablespoons Cointreau or other orange-flavored liqueur

8 to 10 slices egg bread or brioche, crusts removed,
torn into quarter-sized pieces (about 6 cups)

1/3 cup milk

1 tablespoon light molasses

2 eggs

1/2 cup firmly packed brown sugar

1/4 teaspoon salt

2 teaspoons vanilla extract

2 tablespoons apple cider

2 tablespoons coarsely grated orange zest

6 Golden Delicious apples, peeled, cored, and coarsely grated

Confectioners' sugar for dusting

CRÈME CHANTILLY

1 cup crème fraîche, or 1 cup heavy cream
mixed with 2 tablespoons of apple cider vinegar
at room temperature for 1 hour

2 tablespoons granulated sugar

Preheat an oven to 375°F. Using 1 tablespoon of the butter, grease eight 6-ounce ramekins. Put the raisins in a small bowl and pour the liqueur over them. Put the bread pieces in a large bowl.

In a small saucepan, heat the milk and the remaining 4 tablespoons of butter until bubbles just form around the edge, 2 to 3 minutes. Stir in the molasses and remove from heat. Let cool to room temperature.

In a bowl, lightly whisk the eggs, then add the brown sugar, milk mixture, salt, vanilla, apple cider, and orange zest. Whisk together to blend well, then pour this mixture over the bread. Add the grated apples and the raisins and liqueur. Mix well with a

spoon, then spoon into the prepared ramekins.

Bake for 45 minutes, or until the puddings are browned, the sides begin to pull away slightly from the edges, and a toothpick inserted into the center of a pudding comes out clean.

Transfer the ramekins to a wire rack to cool for 10 to 15 minutes, then run a knife along the inside edge of each pudding, unmold each onto a serving plate, and dust with confectioners' sugar.

To make the Crème Chantilly: In a deep bowl, whip the crème fraîche until soft peaks form, then stir in the sugar. Spoon a little onto each pudding and serve warm. *Serves 8*

Croissant Bread Pudding with Fig Sauce

THIS LIGHT AND FLUFFY BREAD PUDDING TOPPED WITH RICH DARK-BROWN FIG SAUCE

MAKES A PERFECT HOLIDAY DESSERT FOR A CASUAL MEAL.

6 to 8 day-old croissants

2 cups milk

2 eggs

1-1/2 cups granulated sugar

1 teaspoon vanilla extract

2 tablespoons butter

1/4 cup dried currants

SAUCE

1 cup dried chopped figs

2 cups boiling water

2 tablespoons firmly packed brown sugar

2 tablespoons rum

Preheat an oven to 350°F. Tear the croissants into bite-sized pieces and put them in a bowl. Pour the milk over them and set aside. In a bowl, combine the eggs and 1 cup of the granulated sugar, and beat until well blended, about 1 minute. Using your hands, squeeze the milk from the croissants and put them in a bowl. Add the squeezed milk to the eggs and sugar, beating briefly. Stir in the vanilla.

With 1 teaspoon of the butter, grease a loaf pan or a deep 8-cup baking dish. Using one third of the croissants, form a layer, then sprinkle with some of the currants and a few dots of the remaining butter. Repeat 2 times. Pour the milk and egg mixture over all, slipping a wooden spoon along the sides of the pan so the liquid penetrates to the bottom. Dot with the remaining butter and sprinkle with the remaining 1/2 cup sugar.

Bake the pudding for about 45 minutes, or until it is puffed and golden brown, the sides have pulled away slightly from the edges of the pan, and a toothpick inserted in the center comes out clean.

To make the sauce: Put the figs in a saucepan, pour the boiling water over them, and let them stand for about 5 minutes. Place over medium heat, add the brown sugar, and bring to a boil, stirring. Reduce heat to low and simmer for about 15 minutes, or until the sauce has thickened and is reduced by about one-third. Stir in the rum and cook another 1 to 2 minutes.

To serve, scoop the warm bread pudding into individual serving bowls and spoon a little warm sauce over each. *Serves 6 to 8*

Caramelized Pecan Upside-Down Cake

CHOPPED PECANS MINGLE WITH BUTTER AND SUGAR TO MAKE A RICH, CARAMELIZED TOPPING WHEN THIS CAKE IS UNMOLDED. SERVE IT WARM, WITH A GENEROUS DOLLOP OF WHIPPED CREAM.

5 tablespoons plus 1 tablespoon butter

3/4 cup firmly packed brown sugar

1-1/2 cup coarsely chopped pecans

4 eggs

1 teaspoon almond extract

1 cup all-purpose flour

1 teaspoon baking powder

1/4 teaspoon salt

1 cup granulated sugar

Preheat an oven to 350°F. Put the 5 tablespoons butter in a 10-inch round baking dish. Put it in the oven for 4 to 5 minutes to melt the butter. Add the brown sugar, stir, and return to the oven for 6 to 7 minutes, stirring once or twice until the sugar has dissolved to form a syrup. Remove from the oven and sprinkle the pecans evenly over the melted butter mixture.

Separate the eggs, breaking the whites into a large bowl and the yolks into a medium bowl. Whisk the 1 tablespoon butter and the almond extract into the egg yolks and set aside. Sift the flour, baking powder, and salt together into a medium bowl. Set aside.

With an electric beater or whisk, beat the egg whites just until they form stiff, glossy peaks. Do not overbeat. Fold the sugar into the egg whites about 1/4 cup at a time. Fold in the egg yolk mixture about one-fourth at a time. Finally, fold in the flour mixture about 1/4 cup at a time. Pour the batter over the pecans and spread with a spatula to cover.

Bake for 30 minutes, or until a toothpick inserted into the center comes out clean.

Remove from the oven and let stand at least 10 minutes before unmolding. The sides will have pulled away slightly. To unmold, run a knife around the edges, then place a large plate or platter over the top of the baking dish. Holding the plate and dish tightly together (remember, the dish is still hot), flip them over so the dish is on top. The cake will fall onto the plate. *Makes one 10-inch cake; serves 6 to 8*

Warm Chocolate Cake

THIS IS PURE CHOCOLATE FLAVOR, SWEET, SMOOTH, AND RICH, WITH A SLIGHTLY SOFT CENTER.

FOR A FANCIFUL DECORATION, USE A STENCIL OR DOILY AND SPRINKLE CONFECTIONERS' SUGAR OR COCOA POWDER

OVER IT TO MAKE THE DESIGN. A CAKE FOR MANY MOODS, THIS CAN BE SERVED PLAIN, WITH ICE CREAM

SUCH AS BLACK WALNUT, OR WITH CRÈME FRAÎCHE OR A RASPBERRY SAUCE.

1 teaspoon butter plus 3/4 cup (1-1/2 sticks), softened

1 cup plus 2 tablespoons all-purpose flour

1/4 teaspoon salt

1-1/2 cups granulated sugar

3 eggs, lightly beaten

2/3 cup unsweetened cocoa powder

3 tablespoons canola oil

1 teaspoon vanilla extract

Preheat an oven to 350°F. Using the 1 teaspoon butter, grease an 8-inch round cake pan that has a swivel arm for easy cake removal, or heavily butter and flour parchment paper for pan lining.

In a small bowl, combine the flour and salt. In a large bowl, using an electric mixer on medium speed, beat the remaining butter until it is creamy, about 1 minute. Gradually blend in the sugar, then add the eggs, beating until smooth and fluffy, about 1 minute. In a small bowl, combine the cocoa and oil, stirring until well blended and smooth. Add the cocoa mixture and the vanilla to the butter mixture and beat just to blend. Add the flour mixture in two or three increments, beating well each time. Spread the mixture evenly into the greased pan.

Bake for 20 minutes, or until a toothpick inserted into the center comes out clean. Transfer the pan to a wire rack to cool for about 10 minutes. Remove the cake from the pan and put it on a cake plate. Decorate if desired. Cut into wedges and serve warm.

Makes one 8-inch cake; serves 6 to 8

Pumpkin-Hazelnut Cheesecake

EVERYONE LOVES CHEESECAKE AND PUMPKIN, AND HERE THE TWO ARE COMBINED IN A SENSUAL DESSERT,

GARNISHED WITH A SOUR CREAM GLAZE AND A LAYER OF FINELY GROUND HAZELNUTS.

CRUST

Graham crackers, finely ground (2-1/2 cups crumbs)

1 cup (5 ounces) hazelnuts, toasted, skinned and
finely ground (page 101)

1/4 cup granulated sugar

4 to 5 tablespoons butter, melted

FILLING

Two 8-ounce packages cream cheese
at room temperature

3/4 cup firmly packed brown sugar

2 eggs

3-1/3 cups homemade or canned pumpkin purée

1/2 cup heavy cream

1/2 teaspoon freshly ground mace

1 teaspoon minced crystallized ginger

1 teaspoon freshly ground cinnamon

TOPPING

1/2 cup sour cream

1/4 cup granulated sugar

1 to 2 tablespoons milk

1/3 cup hazelnuts, toasted, skinned,
and finely ground

To make the crust: Preheat an oven to 325°F. In a small bowl, combine all the ingredients and mix well. Press the mixture over the bottom of a 9 by 2-1/2-inch round springform pan. Using your fingertips, push all but a thin coating of the cookie mixture toward the sides of the pan. Pressing with your fingertips, make a crust about 1-1/2 inches up the sides of the pan; the edges will be slightly irregular. Bake until lightly browned, about 15 minutes. Let cool thoroughly in the refrigerator before filling.

To make the filling: In a large bowl, combine the cream cheese and brown sugar, and using an electric mixer, beat until well blended. Beat in the eggs, one at a time, until the mixture is smooth and well blended.

In a medium bowl, combine the pumpkin purée, cream, and spices, and using a spoon, mix together until well blended. Add the pumpkin mixture to the cream cheese mixture and mix until well blended. Pour the filling into the crust and bake for 50 minutes, or until the center barely moves when jiggled. Let cool on a wire rack, then refrigerate at least overnight before serving.

To make the topping: In a bowl, combine the sour cream, sugar, and 1 tablespoon milk and mix to make a thick sauce. Add 1 tablespoon more milk if necessary.

To serve, run a knife around the edge of the pan, then release the sides, leaving the bottom of the pan in place. Spread the sour cream topping evenly over the cheesecake and dust the top thoroughly with the toasted hazelnuts. Serve chilled, cut into wedges.
Makes one 9-inch cake; serves 12

Christmas Petits Fours

THESE FANCY LITTLE CAKES ARE QUINTESSENTIAL PARTY AND TEATIME FARE. THEIR HOLIDAY DECORATIONS CAN BE PLAIN OR FANCIFUL: BITS OF CRUSHED PISTACHIO, A WHOLE WALNUT MEAT, CANDIED VIOLETS, OR ROSE PETALS.

2 cups cake flour

2 teaspoons baking powder

1/2 teaspoon salt

2 cups granulated sugar

4 eggs

1/2 teaspoon almond extract

1 cup milk, scalded

GLAZE

2 cups apricot preserves or orange marmalade

ICING

1 cup granulated sugar

1/4 teaspoon cream of tartar

1/2 cup water

1-3/4 to 2 cups confectioners' sugar

1 ounce semisweet chocolate, chopped

Food coloring, as desired

Crushed pistachios, walnut halves, candied violets, and/or rose petals for decoration

—continued on next page—

To make the cakes: Preheat an oven to 350°F. Using parchment or waxed paper, line the bottom of an 11-1/2 by 17-1/2-inch jelly roll pan.

Sift the flour twice, then measure and resift with the baking powder and salt. In a deep, medium bowl, combine the sugar and eggs. Using an electric beater at medium speed, beat until the mixture is very thick and fluffy, about 10 minutes, and until it forms a thick ribbon. Pour the mixture into a large bowl. Sprinkle one-third of the flour mixture on the top and fold in with a spatula. Repeat twice more. Add the almond extract and hot milk and beat vigorously with a wooden spoon until thoroughly blended. The batter will be very thin. Pour it immediately into the prepared pan and bake for 10 to 15 minutes, or until the surface springs back when lightly touched.

Remove from the oven and let cool on a wire rack for 10 minutes. Turn out upside down on a towel dusted with confectioners' sugar. Peel away the paper. Let cool another 10 to 15 minutes. Slice the cake in half vertically.

To make the glaze: In a saucepan, heat the apricot preserves or marmalade over medium-low heat until liquefied. Strain, discarding any chunks. Return to the saucepan and heat, stirring, until thickened, 2 to 3 minutes. Using half of the fruit glaze, spread a thick layer on one half of the cake and set the other cake half on top.

Cut the layered cake into 1-1/2-inch squares, or similarly sized rectangles, triangles, or circles. Set the pieces on a wire rack about 2 inches apart, with a pan or aluminum foil set beneath the rack to catch the drippings. Spoon the remaining fruit galze over them, coating well. Refrigerate for 2 to 3 hours, or until the glaze has set and is firm.

To make the icing: In a heavy, medium saucepan, combine the granulated sugar, cream of tartar, and water and bring to a boil. Do not stir. Insert a candy thermometer in the mixture. When the mixture becomes a syrup and reaches 226°F, remove and let cool to 100°F. Gradually stir in the confectioners' sugar until just barely thickened. The icing should be pourable, yet thick enough to adhere to the cakes. Test by pouring it over a cake. If it isn't thick enough, add more confectioners' sugar. If too thick, thin with a little hot water. Divide the icing among 4 small bowls.

In the top of a double boiler over barely simmering water, melt the chocolate and stir it into one bowl of icing. Add drops of food coloring to the others, as desired, stirring to mix well. Again place the cakes on the rack about 2 inches apart, with a pan or aluminum foil beneath. Using a spoon, pour the icing over each cake, letting it run down the sides to coat. Repeat several times to get a thick, glossy coating. If the icing cools before you are finished, reheat over warm water. Once the cakes are iced, decorate as desired. Let the frosting dry and set. Cover loosely and refrigerate until ready to serve. *Makes 24 to 36 small cakes, depending on size*

Angel Food Cake with Coconut

PURE WHITE ANGEL FOOD CAKE, SWIRLED WITH WHIPPED CREAM AND DUSTED WITH COCONUT FLAKES, IS

A WINTER HOLIDAY VISION. IN MAKING THE CAKE, BE CAREFUL NOT TO OVERBEAT THE EGG WHITES—THEY SHOULD BE

SOFT AND MOIST, NOT DRY AND STIFF. FOR A HOLIDAY SHORTCUT, BUY A READY-MADE CAKE AND DECORATE IT.

1 cup superfine sugar

1 cup cake flour

1/2 teaspoon salt

1-1/4 cups egg whites (10 or 11 large eggs)

1-1/2 teaspoons cream of tartar

1 teaspoon finely grated orange zest

1 teaspoon almond extract

FROSTING

1-1/2 cups heavy cream

3/4 cup superfine sugar

2 cups coconut flakes

Preheat an oven to 350°F. Sift the sugar 3 times onto a sheet of waxed paper. Sift the flour 3 times onto another sheet of waxed paper. In a medium bowl, combine the sifted sugar and flour with the salt and sift together. Set aside.

In a large, clean, dry bowl, whisk the egg whites for about 3 minutes, or until frothy. Add the cream of tartar and then, using an electric mixer on medium speed, beat until moist, soft peaks form. Be careful not to overbeat to the stiff-peak stage. Beat in the orange zest and almond extract.

Dust a little of the flour mixture on top of the egg whites, then fold it in. Repeat, in small portions, until all the dry mixture is folded in, and the mixture is light and airy.

Pour into an ungreased 10-inch angel food cake pan with a removable bottom. Bake for 40 to 45 minutes, or until a toothpick inserted into the top comes out clean.

Immediately place the pan upside down on the pan feet, or invert it on the neck of a bottle. Let cool thoroughly at least 1-1/2 to 2 hours before removing from the pan.

Transfer the cake to a cake plate.

To make the frosting: Using an electric beater on medium-high speed, whip the cream until it forms soft peaks. Beat in the sugar until stiff peaks form. Spread the cake top and sides with swirls of whipped cream. Sprinkle generously with coconut flakes, pressing them onto the sides. *Makes one 10-inch cake; serves 12*

Lemon Pound Cake with Warm Poached Cherries

POUND CAKE IS COMFORT FOOD, BUT WHEN COMBINED WITH POACHED CHERRIES, WHICH ARE ESPECIALLY GOOD WITH THE TASTE OF LEMON, IT BECOMES PARTY FOOD FOR GUESTS AS WELL.

1-1/2 teaspoons butter plus 1/2 cup (1 stick), softened

1 cup granulated sugar

2 eggs

Grated zest of 1 lemon

1/2 teaspoon vanilla extract

1/2 teaspoon lemon extract

1-1/2 cups all-purpose flour

1 teaspoon baking powder

1/4 teaspoon salt

1/2 cup milk

CHERRIES

2 cups water

2 cups sugar

2 cups pitted cherries, such as Bing or Queen Anne

1 tablespoon kirsch

Preheat an oven to 350°F. Using the 1-1/2 teaspoons butter, grease a 9 by 5-inch loaf pan. In a large bowl, beat the 1/2 cup butter until it is soft and fluffy. Beat in the sugar until well blended, about 1 minute. Add the eggs one at a time and beat thoroughly after each, until thick and creamy. Beat in the lemon zest and vanilla and lemon extracts.

In a small bowl, combine the flour, baking powder, and salt. Add about one-third of this mixture to the butter mixture and beat until incorporated. Add a little of the milk and beat it in. Repeat until all the flour mixture and milk have been added.

Spread the batter into the prepared pan and bake for about 45 minutes, or until a toothpick inserted into the center comes out clean. Transfer the pan to a wire rack and let the cake cool for 30 minutes.

To cook the cherries: In a medium saucepan, combine the water and sugar and cook over medium heat, stirring, until the sugar has dissolved and a light syrup has formed, 5 to 6 minutes. Add the cherries, reduce heat to medium-low, and simmer for about 15 minutes, or until the cherries are thoroughly softened and the syrup has thickened slightly. Stir in the kirsch. Remove from heat.

To serve, spoon some of the warm cherries and their syrup over a slice of the pound cake. *Serves 6 to 8*

Bite-Sized Dark Rum Fruitcakes

MANY PEOPLE DO NOT LIKE THE BRIGHT RED, GREEN, AND YELLOW CANDIED OR GLACÉED FRUITS FOUND IN FRUITCAKES. IN THIS CAKE, THEY ARE REPLACED BY DRIED FRUITS, SUCH AS APRICOTS AND PRUNES. THE BITE-SIZED CAKES, RICH AND DARK, MAKE GOOD PARTY FARE OR MAY BE USED AS PART OF A MIXED SWEETS TRAY OR HOLIDAY GIFT BOX OF HOME-BAKED SWEETS.

1-1/2 cups all-purpose flour

1/2 teaspoon baking powder

1/4 teaspoon baking soda

1/4 teaspoon salt

1 teaspoon freshly ground cinnamon

1/2 teaspoon freshly grated nutmeg

1/2 teaspoon freshly ground cloves

1/4 teaspoon freshly ground allspice berries

1 cup (2 sticks) butter, softened

1 cup firmly packed dark brown sugar

1/2 cup light molasses

1 egg

1/4 cup dark rum

1/2 cup diced dried apricots

1/2 cup diced pitted prunes

1 cup diced pitted dates

3/4 cups dried currants

3/4 cup raisins

1 cup coarsely chopped walnuts or pecans

Grated zest of 1 orange

Preheat an oven to 300°F. In a medium bowl, combine the flour, baking powder, baking soda, salt, cinnamon, nutmeg, cloves, and allspice and mix well. In a large bowl, using an electric mixer on medium speed, beat the butter until soft and creamy, about 1 minute. Gradually beat in the brown sugar until light and fluffy, 3 to 4 minutes. Beat in the molasses, then the egg, until well blended, about 1 minute. Beat in the flour mixture in thirds, alternating it with the rum, until just blended. With a wooden spoon, stir in the apricots, prunes, dates, currants, raisins, nuts, and orange zest until just blended.

Line a miniature muffin tin with paper liners. Fill each with a heaping tablespoon of batter, about three-fourths full. Bake for 20 minutes or until the cakes spring back when pushed with your finger. Transfer the tin to a wire rack to cool. When completely cool, wrap the cakes in plastic wrap and store in an airtight container for up to 1 month. *Makes about 5 dozen 1-1/2 by 1-inch cakes*

Cranberry-Orange Loaf Cake

CRANBERRIES AND ORANGES ARE A CLASSIC FRUIT COMBINATION, ENHANCED HERE BY DRIED APRICOTS. THIS VERSATILE LOAF IS ESPECIALLY DELICIOUS WHEN SERVED WARM, WITH THE CRANBERRIES STILL HOT. IT MAKES A DELICIOUS TEATIME CAKE EITHER ON ITS OWN, SPREAD WITH GOAT CHEESE, OR WITH A SLICE OF CHEDDAR. TOASTED, IT IS A FINE BREAKFAST BREAD, AND WITH A SCOOP OF ICE CREAM, A TASTY DESSERT.

1 teaspoon butter

1 cup firmly packed light brown sugar

1/2 cup granulated sugar

1/2 teaspoon ground cardamom

1/4 teaspoon ground mace

1-1/2 teaspoons baking powder

1/2 teaspoon baking soda

1/2 teaspoon salt

1/2 cup chopped dried apricots

3/4 cup fresh orange juice, strained

2 tablespoons canola oil

1 egg, beaten

1 cup fresh cranberries, coarsely chopped

Julienned zest of 1/2 orange

Preheat an oven to 350°F. Using the butter, grease a 9-1/2 by 5-inch loaf pan.

In a large bowl, combine the sugars, cardamom, mace, baking powder, baking soda, and salt and mix. Stir in the dried apricots and mix. Pour in the orange juice and oil and stir just to moisten. Stir in the egg, cranberries, and orange zest just until blended.

Spoon into the prepared loaf pan and bake for 45 to 50 minutes, or until the loaf is golden brown on top, pulls away slightly from the edges, and a toothpick inserted into the center comes out clean. Transfer the pan to a wire rack to cool for 15 to 20 minutes, then remove from the pan and put on the rack to cool completely. Once cool, it can be sliced and served, or wrapped in plastic wrap to store overnight. If kept longer than overnight, store in the refrigerator, where it will keep for several days. *Makes 1 loaf; serves 10 to 12*

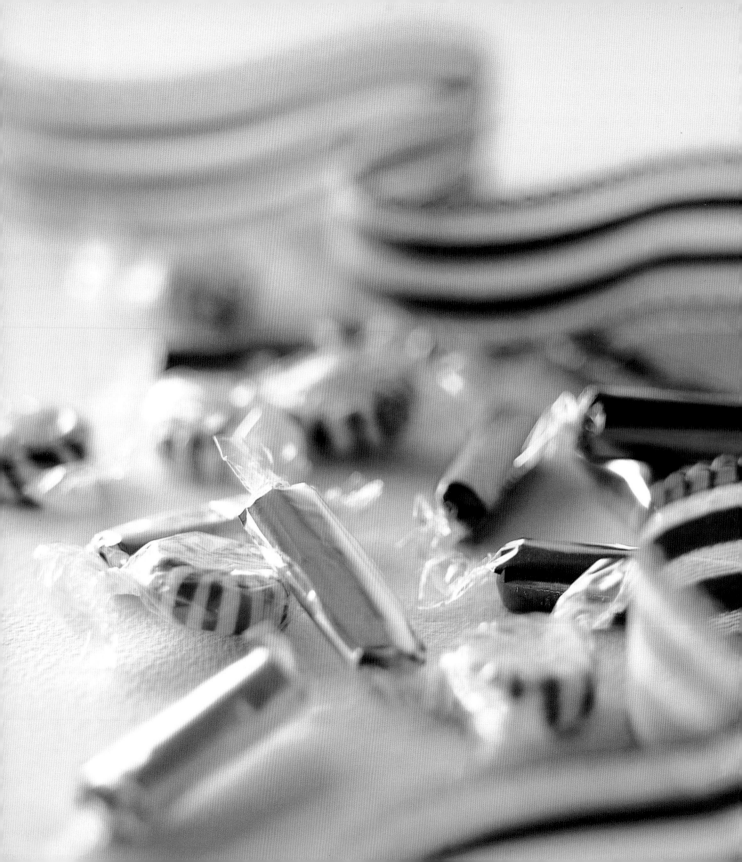

decorative sweets

3

Holiday Candy Wreaths

HOLIDAY WREATHS MADE WITH COLORFUL WRAPPED
CANDIES ARE A DOUBLE DELIGHT: FIRST TO THE EYE AND THEN
TO THE TASTE. VISITORS WILL ENJOY SNATCHING A SWEET
WHEN THEY COME TO CALL, AND MAKING THE WREATHES CAN
BE A FUN FAMILY PROJECT. YOU CAN MAKE WREATHS THAT
ARE COVERED WITH ONLY CANDIES, OR ADD EVERGREEN SPRIGS,
RIBBONS, OR OTHER DECORATIONS AS SHOWN HERE.

YOU WILL NEED:

Evergreen branches and sprigs

20-gauge green florist's wire

Wire wreath frames

Narrow ribbon (optional)

Hot-glue gun and glue sticks

Store-bought wrapped candies

24-inch length of 1-inch-wide decorative ribbon

TO MAKE:

Wrap the stems of the sprigs or small branches with wire, and
wire them to the wreath frame. Cover the stems by placing con-
secutive sprigs over them and wiring them in place, continuing
until the wreath frame is covered.

For a variation, knot 3- to 4-inch pieces of narrow colored
ribbon and space them around the wreath frame.

Put a small dot of glue on the back of the candies and glue
them to the greenery or frame around the wreath in a decorative
pattern.

Loop a 24-inch length of 1-inch wide ribbon through the top
back of the wreath and hang on a door, window, or mirror.

Candied Popcorn Star Ornaments

GARLANDS MADE OF POPCORN HAVE LONG BEEN A TRADITIONAL ADORNMENT FOR HOLIDAY CHRISTMAS TREES. THESE DELICATE POPCORN STAR ORNAMENTS ARE A LOVELY VARIATION OF THIS OLD DECORATIVE FAVORITE. CREATE STAR VARIATIONS BY USING PLAIN AND CANDIED POPCORN, OR BY VARYING THE LENGTH AND NUMBER OF THE STAR POINTS. CHILDREN WILL ENJOY THIS PROJECT TOO, BUT BE SURE TO PREPARE EXTRA POPCORN FOR SNACKING.

YOU WILL NEED:

Plain or candy-coated popcorn for Popcorn Balls
(see recipe page 72)

20-gauge wire

Hot-glue gun and glue sticks

Unpopped popcorn, fresh cranberries, or
dried seed pods

8-inch lengths of ribbon or decorative cord

TO MAKE:

Prepare the Popcorn Ball recipe up to the point that the balls are shaped. For each star, cut 4 to 6 pieces of wire into 4- to 6-inch lengths and thread popcorn onto the wire pieces. Using 2 pieces of wire, make a cross and twist the wires around each other at the centers. Continue adding popcorn to the wires, twisting them at the center. Remove the popcorn at the center of the intersections to achieve a flat center.

Glue popcorn kernels, cranberries, or seed pods in the center of the stars and tie ribbon or cord to the end of a star point for hanging.

Candy Acorn Kissing Ball

KISSING BALLS ARE TRADITIONALLY MADE OF MISTLETOE BUT CAN BE CREATED WITH A VARIETY OF SEASONAL GREENERY SUCH AS IVY, BOXWOOD, OR EUCALYPTUS. THIS UNUSUAL BALL IS STUDDED WITH BEAUTIFULLY WRAPPED, ACORN-SHAPED CHOCOLATES THAT CAN BE PLUCKED BY THOSE WHO CRAVE A SWEET ALONG WITH A KISS.

YOU WILL NEED:

Eucalyptus pods and foliage

6-inch Styrofoam ball

Hot-glue gun and glue sticks

Foil-wrapped candy acorns or
other decorative wrapped candy

24-inch length of 2-inch-wide satin ribbon

U-shaped 2-inch floral pin

12-inch length of 2-inch-wide satin ribbon

TO MAKE:

Insert the stems of the pods into the Styrofoam ball, securing them with dabs of glue, until the ball is covered. Insert small stems of foliage between the seed pods. Glue candies directly onto the greenery on all sides of the ball.

Thread the longer ribbon halfway through the floral pin and tie a knot around the pin. Insert the pin into the top of the ball. Secure by dabbing hot glue around the pin.

Tie the short ribbon into a bow and glue the underside of the knot to the greenery at the top of the ball. Hang the ball by the ribbon over a doorway or mirror.

Stenciled Gingerbread Cookie Box

THIS ELEGANT GINGERBREAD COOKIE BOX IS A BEAUTIFUL WAY TO PRESENT HOMEMADE HOLIDAY COOKIES TO FAMILY AND FRIENDS.

YOU WILL NEED:

Lightweight cardboard

Ruler

Pencil

Tracing paper

X-Acto knife

Compass

Gingerbread dough (see recipe page 74)

1/4 cup corn syrup in small bowl

Small, unused paintbrush

Confectioners' sugar

Fine meshed tea strainer or small sieve

1 small tube store-bought white cookie icing

Silver dragées

12-inch length of 1/4-inch-wide silver ribbon for box handle

Decorative cake plate or tray

TO MAKE:

Draw and cut out a 3-by-5-inch rectangle of cardboard for the box sides. Trace a leaf stencil onto the tracing paper and transfer onto the center of the cardboard rectangle. Using the X-Acto knife, carefully cut out the outline. Using the compass, draw a 10-inch diameter circle on the cardboard, then draw a hexagon inside the circle and cut out for the box top.

Preheat the oven to 375°F. Prepare the gingerbread dough and roll it out 1/4-inch thick on a work surface covered with waxed paper. Using the rectangular template, cut out 6 rectangles for the box sides and transfer the sides to a buttered baking sheet. Gather the dough scraps and roll out the remaining dough. Using the hexagonal template, mark and cut out the box top. Cut a 3/8-inch slit in the center of the top for the handle. Triple-fold a 3/8-inch piece of aluminum foil and wedge it in the slit to keep it open. Transfer the top to the baking sheet and bake for 15 minutes. Remove and let cool on a wire rack.

Place the leaf stencil on top of a box side and brush lightly with corn syrup. Do not remove the template and let dry for 10 minutes. Place 2 tablespoons confectioners' sugar in the strainer or sieve and tap lightly to sprinkle sugar over the stencil leaves. Remove the template carefully and repeat for each side.

Using the icing, make a row of tiny dots along the top and bottom edges of the box sides and place a silver dragée on each dot. Repeat along the edges of the box top.

Fold the ribbon in half, thread the loop end through the slit, and knot it on the underside of the box top. Select a cake plate or tray with a flat bottom. Place the cardboard box-top template in the center of the plate. Draw a line of icing along the inside of a short edge of one of the box sides. Stand the side upright along the template edge and fit another box side to the iced edge. Repeat until all sides are iced together on the template. Let dry for 30 minutes. Fill with cookies and place the top on the box.

cookies & candies

Pecan Lace Cookies

THESE DELICATE BUT RICH, CRISPY COOKIES ARE QUICK AND EASY TO MAKE. WALNUTS, PISTACHIOS, OR HAZELNUTS MIGHT BE USED AS WELL. FOR AN EXTRA-FANCY ELEMENT, WHILE THE COOKIES ARE STILL WARM AND PLIABLE, WRAP THEM AROUND THE HANDLE OF A WOODEN SPOON. THE ENDS CAN ALSO BE DIPPED IN MELTED CHOCOLATE, IF DESIRED, OR TWO COOKIES CAN BE PUT TOGETHER, SANDWICH-STYLE, WITH CHOCOLATE ICING.

1/2 cup (1 stick) unsalted butter

3/4 cup firmly packed brown sugar

1 tablespoon molasses

1 tablespoon light corn syrup

3/4 cups quick-cooking rolled oats

1/4 cup finely chopped pecans, toasted

1-1/2 tablespoons all-purpose flour

1/4 teaspoon salt

1 teaspoon vanilla extract

Preheat an oven to 350°F. In a heavy saucepan, melt the butter over medium heat. When it foams, add the brown sugar, stirring until it dissolves, 2 to 3 minutes. Stir in the molasses and corn syrup, then the oats, pecans, flour, salt, and vanilla. Stir until well blended. Remove from heat and drop teaspoonfuls onto a parchment or aluminum foil-lined baking sheet at least 2 inches apart, as the cookies will spread during cooking. Bake for 7 to 9 minutes, or until the cookies are golden brown and the edges slightly darker.

Remove from the oven and let cool on the pan for 4 to 5 minutes, or until slightly firmed. With a metal spatula, transfer the cookies to wire racks. If desired, while still pliable, form them around the handle of a wooden spoon. *Makes about 48 cookies*

Apricot-Pistachio Bars

THESE SOFT, ALMOST CHEWY BARS ARE REDOLENT WITH THE SCENTS OF THE MIDDLE EAST: PISTACHIOS, APRICOTS, CARDAMOM, AND MACE. THEY ARE TARTLY SWEET AND RATHER CAKELIKE, AN UNUSUAL ADDITION TO ANY HOLIDAY COOKIE LIST.

1 teaspoon butter plus 1 cup (2 sticks), softened

1/2 cup granulated sugar

1/2 cup firmly packed light brown sugar

4 eggs

1 tablespoon grated orange zest

1/2 teaspoon vanilla extract

1 teaspoon apricot brandy (optional)

1-1/4 cups all-purpose flour

1 teaspoon baking powder

1/2 teaspoon baking soda

1/2 teaspoon ground cardamom

1/4 teaspoon ground mace

2 cups coarsely chopped dried apricots

1/2 cup dried currants

1/2 cup coarsely chopped pistachios

ICING

1-1/2 cups confectioners' sugar

2 to 3 tablespoons orange juice

Preheat an oven to 350°F. Using the 1 teaspoon butter, grease a 10 by 15-inch baking pan.

In a large bowl, beat the 1 cup butter and the sugars until light and fluffy. Beat in the eggs one at a time, blending well. Add the orange zest, vanilla, and apricot brandy and beat to blend well.

In a medium bowl, combine the flour, baking powder, baking soda, cardamom, mace, apricots, currants, and pistachios and stir to mix well. Stir the flour mixture into the butter mixture and blend well. Spread the batter evenly in the prepared pan and bake for about 20 minutes, or until a toothpick inserted in the center comes out clean. Transfer the pan to a wire rack and let cool about 15 minutes.

To make the icing: In a bowl, combine the confectioners' sugar and orange juice and mix to a medium-firm consistency. Spread on the top of the still-warm, uncut cookies in the pan and let stand until the icing sets. Cut the cookies into 1-1/2-inch squares.

To store, place in single layers, separated by sheets of waxed paper, in an airtight container. Store for 2 to 3 days, or freeze.
Makes 65 to 70 cookies

Frosted Ornament Cookies

IT WOULDN'T BE THE HOLIDAYS WITHOUT FROSTED COOKIES. ORNAMENTS OF ALL SHAPES ARE ESPECIALLY FUN
TO MAKE, EITHER AS EDIBLE TREATS FOR THE TREE OR SIMPLY FOR THE COOKIE PLATE.

1-3/4 cups sifted all-purpose flour

1/2 teaspoon baking powder

1/4 teaspoon salt

2/3 cup (1-1/3 sticks) butter, softened

1/2 cup granulated sugar

1 egg

1 teaspoon vanilla extract

FROSTING

Confectioners' sugar

Milk

Food coloring as needed

Silver dragées (optional)

Colored sugars (optional)

Preheat an oven to 400°F. In a sifter, combine the flour, the baking powder, and salt and sift onto a piece of waxed paper. In a large bowl, beat the butter and sugar together until light and fluffy. Beat in the egg and vanilla, then add the flour mixture in thirds, stirring each time until the dough is smooth.

On a lightly floured board, roll the dough out to a thickness of 1/8 inch. Cut into the desired cookie shapes and transfer them to an ungreased baking sheet. For cookie ornaments to hang on a tree, make a 1/4-inch-diameter hole in each cookie with the blunt end of a wooden skewer. Gather up the scraps of dough and roll them out to use all the dough. Bake just until lightly browned on the bottom and pale golden on top, 6 to 8 minutes. Let the cookies cool on the pan for 5 minutes, then transfer them to wire racks.

To make the frosting: In a medium bowl, combine the confectioners' sugar and milk and stir until a stiff but spreadable paste forms. (It may seem overly stiff, but too much milk will make an unworkable frosting. If it is necessary to add more milk, do so only 1/2 teaspoon at a time.) Divide the frosting among separate bowls and mix in coloring as desired. Frost the cookies while they are warm or cool. If the cookies are warm, the frosting will spread more easily. Add decorative silver dragées and colored sugars if desired before the frosting dries. *Makes about 36 cookies*

Grandma's Molasses Cookies

CRUNCHY AND CRISP, LIGHT AND AIRY, WITH A DELICATE TASTE OF MOLASSES,
THESE ARE THE COOKIES CHILDREN KEEP COMING BACK FOR OVER AND OVER AGAIN.

3/4 cup (1-1/2 sticks) unsalted butter

1 cup granulated sugar

1/4 cup molasses

1 egg, lightly beaten

2 cups all-purpose flour

2 teaspoons baking soda

1/2 teaspoon freshly ground cloves

1/2 teaspoon ground ginger

1 teaspoon freshly ground cinnamon

1/4 teaspoon salt

Preheat an oven to 375°F. In a saucepan, melt the butter over medium heat, stirring frequently, 3 to 4 minutes. Remove and let cool to room temperature. Pour it into a large bowl and stir in 3/4 cup of sugar, molasses, and egg until well blended. Stir in the flour, baking soda, cloves, ginger, cinnamon, and salt and mix well. Cover and refrigerate for 30 minutes.

Sprinkle a sheet of waxed paper with the remaining 1/4 cup sugar. Tear off pieces of dough about the size of walnuts and form them into 1-inch balls. Roll the balls in the sugar and place them about 1-1/2 inches apart on a baking sheet.

Bake for 10 minutes, or until the cookies puff up, then settle back down. Transfer the cookies to a wire rack and let cool. To store, place in single layers, separated by waxed paper in an airtight container. *Makes about 48 cookies*

Old-Fashioned Peanut Brittle

ANY CLASSIC RECIPE HAS DOZENS OF VARIATIONS, AND PEANUT BRITTLE IS NO EXCEPTION.
THIS VERSION IS OPAQUE, WITH A BUTTERY TASTE THAT MAKES IT HARD TO STOP EATING. IF YOU WISH,
REPLACE THE PEANUTS WITH PECANS, WALNUTS, ALMONDS, OR OTHER NUTS.

2 teaspoons plus 3 tablespoons butter

1-1/2 teaspoons baking soda

1 teaspoon plus 1 cup water

1 teaspoon vanilla extract

1 cup light corn syrup

1-1/2 cups granulated sugar

1 pound unsalted, roasted peanuts

Preheat an oven to 250°F. Using the 2 teaspoons butter, grease two 12 by 15-inch baking sheets and place them in the oven.

In a small bowl, combine the baking soda, the 1 teaspoon water, and the vanilla and set aside. In a large saucepan, combine the 1 cup water, the corn syrup, and sugar. Insert a candy thermometer into the sugar mixture and cook over medium heat, stirring to dissolve the sugar, for 4 to 5 minutes, or until the mixture is clear and the thermometer reads 240°F.

Stir in the 3 tablespoons butter and the peanuts and cook, stirring constantly, until the mixture has thickened and the thermometer reads 300°F. Be careful that it doesn't burn.

Remove from the heat and immediately stir in the baking soda mixture. Remove the baking sheets from the oven. Pour half the candy mixture onto each warm baking sheet and quickly spread evenly about 1/4 inch thick.

Set aside to cool for about 1 hour. When cool, lift the edges of the brittle and break it into pieces. To store, pack in single layers, separated by waxed paper, in airtight containers. It will keep for up to 1 month. *Makes about 2 pounds*

Turkish Delight

THESE ARE THE JELLY CANDIES GIVEN OUT BY THE SNOW QUEEN IN C. S. LEWIS'S CLASSIC TALE *THE LION, THE WITCH AND THE WARDROBE*. UNABLE TO RESIST THE SWEET, EDMUND ALLOWED HIMSELF TO FALL UNDER THE SPELL OF THE WHITE WITCH AND IS SPIRITED OFF TO HER ICY CASTLE. THESE ARE A FAVORITE TREAT IN THE MIDDLE EAST, OFTEN FLAVORED WITH ROSE WATER.

2 tablespoons water

3/4 cup plus 1 tablespoon liquid pectin

1/2 teaspoon baking soda

1-1/4 cups light corn syrup

3/4 cup granulated sugar

1 teaspoon cherry, mint, or orange extract

Food coloring as desired

1 tablespoon fresh lemon juice

Confectioners' sugar for dusting

In a large saucepan, combine the water and pectin, then stir in the baking soda. The mixture will foam and become frothy. In another large saucepan, combine the corn syrup and sugar.

Place both saucepans over high heat and bring to a boil, cooking for 4 to 5 minutes and stirring both constantly. When the pectin mixture has stopped foaming and the sugar mixture is boiling, gradually pour the pectin mixture into the sugar mixture, stirring constantly. While continuing to stir, bring back to a boil and boil for 1 minute. Add the extract and food coloring.

Remove from heat and stir in the lemon juice. Pour into an 8-inch-square glass baking dish and let stand for 3 to 4 hours, or until set and firm.

Cut into 1-inch squares and remove them from the pan. Dust the squares thoroughly with confectioners' sugar and place them on wire racks to dry for at least 12 hours or up to 18 hours. To store, dust again with confectioners' sugar on all sides and pack in layers, separated by waxed paper, in an airtight tin. It will keep for up to 3 weeks. *Makes 64 squares*

Almond-Butter Toffee

BRUSHED WITH CHOCOLATE AND CRUNCHY WITH ALMONDS AND PECANS,

THIS CANDY MAKES A VERY SPECIAL HOLIDAY GIFT.

1 tablespoon plus 1-1/4 cups
(2-1/2 sticks) butter

2-1/4 cups granulated sugar

1 teaspoon salt

1/2 cup water

1-1/2 cups coarsely ground blanched almonds

1 cup chopped pecans

Four 1 ounce squares semisweet chocolate

Using the 1 tablespoon butter, grease a 15 by 17-inch jelly roll pan. In a saucepan combine the remaining 1-1/4 cups butter, the sugar, salt, and water and bring to a boil over high heat, stirring. Stir in 3/4 cup of the almonds and insert a candy thermometer in the mixture. Continue to cook, stirring constantly until the thermometer reads 312°F. At this point, the candy will turn brown and start to pull away from the sides of the pan. Stir in the remaining almonds and the pecans. Pour into the prepared pan and let cool for about 1 hour, or until hard.

In the top of a double boiler, melt the chocolate over barely simmering water, stirring. Remove from heat and spread the chocolate on the candy. Let cool for at least 30 minutes or up to several hours. Lift the toffee from the edges of the pan and break into pieces. To store, pack in single layers, separated by waxed paper, in an airtight container. The toffee will keep for up to 10 days.
Makes about 8 dozen 1-1/2-inch squares

Chocolate Fudge

FUDGES ARE THE QUINTESSENTIAL RICH CANDY, AND EVERYONE HAS A FAVORITE VERSION, WITH OR WITHOUT NUTS. FOR SPECIAL HOLIDAY GIFTS, PACK A SELECTION IN A COLORFUL CANDY TIN LINED WITH WAXED PAPER AND TIED WITH A PRETTY RIBBON.

1 teaspoon plus 4 tablespoons melted butter

1 cup firmly packed light brown sugar

1 cup granulated sugar

1/4 cup light corn syrup

1/2 cup half-and-half

1/8 teaspoon salt

4 tablespoons Dutch-processed, unsweetened cocoa powder

1 teaspoon vanilla extract

1/2 cup chopped pecans or walnuts (optional)

Using the 1 teaspoon of butter, grease an 8-inch square pan and set aside. In a large saucepan, combine the 4 tablespoons butter, the sugars, corn syrup, half-and-half, and salt and cook over medium-high heat, stirring constantly. Using a pastry brush dipped in hot water, remove any sugar crystals that form on the sides of the saucepan. When the mixture boils, cook for 2-1/2 minutes, then add the cocoa, stirring until well blended. Insert a candy thermometer into the mixture and continue to boil, without stirring, for 7 to 10 minutes, or until the thermometer reads 234°F.

Remove from the heat, add the vanilla, and let cool for 5 minutes, or until the thermometer reads 110°F. Beat with a wooden spoon or electric beater until the fudge is creamy and the color dulls, 2 or 3 minutes. Mix in the chopped nuts by hand, if desired. Pour the fudge into the prepared pan, smoothing the top evenly. Cover and refrigerate for 24 hours.

To serve, cut into squares. To store, place in single layers, separated by waxed paper, in an airtight container. *Makes about 5 dozen 1-inch squares*

Pecan Penuche

PENUCHE IS VERY SIMILAR IN TASTE AND CONSISTENCY TO PRALINES. IT IS OFTEN CUT INTO SMALL
SQUARES LIKE FUDGE AND MAKES A DELICIOUS ADDITION TO HOLIDAY CANDY GIFT TINS. FOR A STRONGER PECAN FLAVOR,
THE NUTS CAN BE TOASTED IN THE OVEN ON A BAKING SHEET AT 350°F FOR 10 TO 12 MINUTES.

1 teaspoon plus 3 tablespoons butter

2-1/4 cups firmly packed light brown sugar

3/4 cup half-and-half

1/8 teaspoon salt

1 teaspoon vanilla extract

1/2 cup chopped pecans

Using the 1 teaspoon butter, grease an 8-inch square baking pan. In a large saucepan, combine the brown sugar, half-and-half, and salt. Cook, stirring constantly, over medium-high heat until the mixture boils. Using a pastry brush dipped in hot water, remove any sugar crystals that form on the sides of the saucepan. Cook for 2-1/2 minutes. Insert a candy thermometer into the mixture and continue to boil, without stirring, for 4 to 5 minutes, or until the thermometer reads 238°F.

Remove from the heat and add the remaining 3 tablespoons butter, but do not stir. Let cool for 5 minutes, or until the thermometer reads 110°F. Add the vanilla and beat with a wooden spoon until the mixture begins to thicken. Add the nuts and beat until the penuche is creamy and the color dulls, 2 to 3 minutes. Pour it into the prepared pan, smoothing the top evenly. Cover and refrigerate for 24 hours.

To serve, cut into squares. To store, place in single layers, separated by waxed paper, in an airtight container. *Makes about 30 1-1/2-inch squares*

Hazelnut Divinity

THE ADDITION OF EGG WHITES TO THIS BASIC SUGAR CANDY SYRUP MAKES A FIRM BUT CREAMY CANDY. VANILLA AND TOASTED HAZELNUTS GIVE IT A DELICIOUS NUTTY FLAVOR. FOR A CHRISTMASTIME VARIATION, SUBSTITUTE 1 CUP CRUSHED PEPPERMINT CANDY.

3 cups granulated sugar

1/2 cup light corn syrup

1/8 teaspoon salt

2/3 cup water

2 egg whites

1 teaspoon vanilla extract

1 cup hazelnuts, toasted, skinned, and
coarsely chopped (see page 101)

Line a baking sheet with waxed paper and set aside. In a large saucepan, combine the sugar, corn syrup, salt, and water. Cook over medium-high heat, stirring constantly, until the mixture boils. Using a pastry brush dipped in hot water, remove any sugar crystals that form on the sides of the saucepan. Insert a candy thermometer into the mixture and cook without stirring until the thermometer reads 250°F, about 6 to 7 minutes.

In a large bowl, beat the egg whites until stiff, glossy peaks form. While beating constantly, slowly pour the hot syrup into the beaten egg whites, and continue to beat until the mixture loses its glossy appearance and forms stiff peaks, 10 to 15 minutes. Stir in the vanilla and nuts and mix until well blended. Dip a tablespoon in hot water, then scoop up a heaping tablespoon of the mixture and push it off the spoon onto the waxed paper. Repeat until all the mixture is used. Set aside to cool and become firm, about 30 minutes. Once firm, remove the candies from the waxed paper with a metal spatula. To store, place in single layers, separated by waxed paper, in an airtight container. *Makes about 30 candies*

sweet gifts

5

Cookie Cup Gifts

EVERYONE LOVES THE COMFORT OF TEA AND COOKIES. THIS SIMPLE WRAP COMBINES

THE TWO AND MAKES A WONDERFUL GIFT FOR A NEIGHBOR OR CO-WORKER.

YOU WILL NEED:

Cookies

Waxed paper or parchment paper

Large, oversized cup and saucer

Decorative ribbon

Gift tags

TO MAKE:

Wrap the cookies in the waxed or parchment paper. Place them
in the cup and tie a ribbon around the cup, saucer, and cookies.
Add a gift tag.

Bamboo Steamer Cookie Baskets

DELICATE, ROUND BAMBOO STEAMER BASKETS MAKE AN UNUSUAL
AND USEFUL PACKAGE FOR A COLLECTION OF HOMEMADE HOLIDAY COOKIES.

YOU WILL NEED:

Pencil

Tiered bamboo steamer baskets

Waxed paper

Scissors

Assorted cookies

Ribbon

Gift tags

Holiday decorations or ornaments

TO MAKE:

With a pencil, trace the circumference of each basket on waxed paper, adding 2 inches to the diameter. Cut out with scissors and line the bottom of each basket.

Pack each basket with cookies and put an extra piece of waxed paper over the top tier. Put on the basket top.

Tie the tiers together at the top with the ribbon. Add a gift tag and decorations.

Cookie Cutter Gifts

CHILDREN AND ADULTS ALIKE WILL DELIGHT IN THE NOVELTY OF A GIFT OF COOKIE CUTTERS WITH COOKIES INSIDE. BECAUSE THE COOKIES ARE BAKED INSIDE THE COOKIE CUTTERS TO RETAIN THEIR ORIGINAL SIZE, YOU WILL NEED SEVERAL CUTTERS OF THE SAME SHAPE. BE SURE TO INCLUDE THE RECIPE ON A CARD.

YOU WILL NEED:

Gingerbread dough (page 74)

Several large copper or aluminum cookie cutters

Ribbon

Gift tags

TO MAKE:

Preheat an oven to 375°F. Prepare the dough. Roll out the dough onto a well-floured surface. Using the cookie cutters, cut out cookies of each shape and transfer to a buttered or parchment-lined baking pan.

Place each cookie cutter over a cookie on the sheet and bake the cookies according to the recipe. Let all the cookies cool completely on the pan (don't remove the cutters).

Stack several cookies inside each cutter and tie together with a ribbon. Attach a gift tag.

Decorative Pudding or Fruitcake Gifts

MAKING COLLAGE-STYLE TINS AND LINED BASKETS FOR HOMEMADE PUDDINGS AND CAKES, THEN TYING

THEM WITH SPECIAL RIBBONS, ADDS A VERY PERSONAL TOUCH TO YOUR GIFTS.

YOU WILL NEED:

Decorative paper

Scissors

Paintbrush

White glue

Fruit cake loaf pans, tin pudding molds,
or wire baskets

Parchment paper

Loaf fruitcakes (page 29), loaf cakes (page 31),
or plum puddings (page 14)

Adhesive tape

Decorative ribbon

Gift tags

Linen napkin or tea towel

TO MAKE:

Cut the decorative paper into small or medium pieces. Brush the back sides of the paper pieces with white glue and place the paper collage-style all over the pans or molds, inside and out, until completely covered. Let dry.

Cut 4-by-12-inch lengths of parchment paper and wrap the paper bands around the center of each fruitcake or loaf cake. Secure on the underside with tape.

For the puddings, cut out circles of parchment paper 2 inches wider than each pudding. Set a pudding on the paper and fold up the sides. Using a 4-by-12-inch piece of parchment paper, make an overwrapping collar around each pudding and secure with tape. Alternatively, line a decorative wire basket with a special linen napkin or tea towel and set a wrapped pudding into it.

Tie ribbon and gift tags around the pans, tins, or baskets.

sweets for kids

6

Popcorn Balls

STICKY CARAMEL POPCORN BALLS ARE A WONDERFUL HOMEMADE TREAT FOR CHILDREN. IF THE CHILDREN ARE HELPING, BE EXTREMELY CAREFUL BECAUSE THE MELTED SUGAR IS VERY HOT. ONCE THE CARAMELIZED COATING HAS COOLED TO LUKEWARM, THE CHILDREN CAN HELP SHAPE THE BALLS. BE SURE TO TEST IT YOURSELF FIRST.

1-1/4 cups granulated sugar

1-1/2 cups firmly packed brown sugar

3/4 cup light corn syrup

1/4 cup light molasses

1/2 cup water

2 tablespoons butter

1/2 teaspoon salt

1 teaspoon vanilla extract

16 cups popcorn
(approximately 1 cup unpopped)

Line a baking sheet with waxed paper. In a large saucepan, combine the sugars, corn syrup, molasses, and water. Cook over medium heat, stirring constantly, until the sugars are dissolved, 4 to 5 minutes. Insert a candy thermometer in the mixture and continue to cook, stirring constantly, until the temperature reaches 284°F.

Remove from heat and stir in the butter, salt, and vanilla until the butter has melted.

Put the popcorn in a large bowl or pan and pour the sugar syrup over it. Using a wooden spoon, mix it well, then let cool to lukewarm, about 7 to 10 minutes. Butter your hands and shape the popcorn into balls about 2 inches in diameter.

Set the balls on the prepared pan to harden for 1 hour. When hard, wrap them individually in plastic wrap and store in an airtight container, where they will keep for 3 or 4 days. *Makes about 24 balls*

Candied Apples

CANDIED APPLES ARE A FUN HOLIDAY SWEET FOR CHILDREN TO EAT AND TO MAKE. THEY ARE A COLORFUL TREAT TO GIVE TO TRICK-OR-TREATERS, CHRISTMAS CAROLERS, OR YOUNG PARTY GUESTS. KIDS CAN HELP PUT IN THE SKEWERS AND FOOD COLORING AND THEN MAKE FESTIVE CELLOPHANE WRAPPERS WITH STICKERS, HOLIDAY DECORATIONS, AND RIBBON WHILE THE CANDIED APPLES ARE COOLING.

Four 6-inch wooden skewers or popsicle sticks

4 firm red apples such as Rome Beauty or Red Delicious

1 cup granulated sugar

3/4 cup boiling water

Pinch of cream of tartar

Several drops red food coloring

Insert a skewer in each apple. Butter a baking sheet. Prepare a double boiler with water simmering just below the upper pan.

In a small, heavy saucepan, combine the sugar, boiling water, and cream of tartar. Cook over low heat, stirring constantly until the sugar has dissolved, 4 to 5 minutes. Continue to cook, stirring occasionally, until the syrup is boiling, 3 to 4 minutes. Cover and cook for 3 minutes without stirring. Uncover and insert a candy thermometer. When it reads 300°F, remove the pan from heat and pour the hot syrup into the top of the double boiler. Stir in the food coloring.

Working quickly, dip the apples one at a time in the syrup until covered with the glaze. Set each, top-side down, on the prepared baking sheet and let stand for at least 15 minutes or up to several hours to harden.

Wrap in plastic wrap or cellophane and store in an airtight container in a cool, dry location for up to 3 days. *Makes 4 apples*

Candy Cane Cookies

THESE TWO-TONED COOKIES, DELICATELY FLAVORED AND WITH A SOFT, BUTTERY TEXTURE, ARE ESPECIALLY FUN FOR CHILDREN TO MAKE BECAUSE THE DOUGH IS SHAPED BY HAND, JUST LIKE MODELING CLAY.

RED DOUGH

1/2 cup (1 stick) butter, softened

1/3 cup plus 1 tablespoon granulated sugar

1 egg yolk

1/4 teaspoon almond extract

2 teaspoons red food coloring

1-1/4 cups all-purpose flour

PLAIN DOUGH

1/2 cup (1 stick) butter, softened

1/3 cup plus 1 tablespoon granulated sugar

1 egg yolk

1/4 teaspoon almond extract

1-1/4 cups all-purpose flour

Preheat an oven to 425°F. To make the red dough: In a bowl, beat the butter until soft and creamy. Slowly beat in the sugar, and when it is fully incorporated, beat in the egg yolk, almond extract, and food coloring until well blended. Beat in the flour until well blended. Shape the dough into a ball, wrap in plastic wrap, and refrigerate for 15 minutes.

To make the plain dough: Repeat the process for the red dough, omitting the food coloring. Shape into ball, wrap in plastic wrap and refrigerate for 15 minutes.

Tear off a walnut-sized piece of red dough, and using the palms of your hands, roll it out on aluminum foil to form a rope about 1/4 inch in diameter and 5 inches long. Do the same with the plain dough. Twist the ropes together and then bend the top into a curve to make a candy cane. Place on an ungreased baking sheet about 1 inch apart. Repeat until all the dough is used. Bake for about 8 minutes, or until lightly browned on the bottom.

Transfer the cookies to a wire rack to cool. To store, pack in an airtight container in single layers, separated by waxed paper.

Makes about 30 cookies

Gingerbread People

GINGERBREAD PEOPLE ARE VIRTUALLY REQUIRED FOR THE HOLIDAY SEASON, AND THEY ARE EASY TO MAKE. IF CHILDREN HELP, IT IS GREAT FUN. THE IDEAL DOUGH IS SOFT ENOUGH TO ROLL OUT, YET STIFF ENOUGH TO HOLD THE FORMS, RESULTING IN FINISHED COOKIES THAT ARE MOIST BUT NOT CRUMBLY. DECORATE WITH CURRANTS, CRANBERRIES, CANDIES, FROSTING, AND CONFECTIONERS' SUGAR.

1 teaspoon plus 1/2 cup (1 stick) butter, softened

1/2 cup firmly packed light brown sugar

1/2 cup light molasses

3 cups all-purpose flour

1 teaspoon baking soda

1/4 teaspoon freshly ground cloves

1/2 teaspoon freshly ground cinnamon

1/2 teaspoon freshly grated nutmeg

1 teaspoon ground ginger

1/2 teaspoon salt

1/4 to 1/3 cup milk

Dried currants, red-hots, fresh or dried cranberries, and silver dragées for decorating

Frosting (page 49) and confectioners' sugar

Preheat an oven to 350°F. Using the 1 teaspoon butter, grease a large baking sheet.

In a large bowl, beat the 1/2 cup butter and the sugar until light and fluffy. Beat in the molasses until well blended. In a medium bowl, combine the flour, baking soda, cloves, cinnamon, nutmeg, ginger, and salt.

Add half of the flour mixture to the butter mixture and beat until well blended. Beat in about 1/4 cup milk, then add the remaining flour mixture, beating it in well. The dough will be very stiff. If it is too stiff and crumbly to roll out, add 1 tablespoon of additional milk.

On a well-floured surface, roll the dough out to a thickness of about 1/2 inch, then cut into shapes using cookie cutters or by tracing with a knife around cardboard cutouts. Transfer the shapes to the prepared pan.

Decorate the gingerbread people with currant eyes and red-hots for buttons, pressing them into the dough before baking, or attach them with frosting after baking.

Bake for 7 to 8 minutes, or until the cookies are puffed and spring back when pushed with your finger. Transfer the cookies from the pan to a wire rack to cool. Decorate with frosting as desired. *Makes about sixteen 4-inch cookies*

Holiday Thumbprint Cookies

NOT ONLY ARE THESE ABOUT THE EASIEST COOKIES TO MAKE, BUT THEY ALSO OFFER A GREAT VARIATION IN ORNAMENTAL IDEAS. BITS OF CANDIED CHERRY, SINGLE NUTS, COCONUT, OR A DOLLOP OF JAM OR MELTED CHOCOLATE CAN ALL BE USED FOR DECORATION.

1/2 cup (1 stick) butter, softened

1/2 cup firmly packed light brown sugar

1 egg

1/2 teaspoon vanilla extract

1/4 teaspoon grated lime zest

1 cup all-purpose flour

1/4 teaspoon salt

1/4 to 1/3 cup finely ground almonds, walnuts, or hazelnuts

Seedless jam, chocolate chips, candied cherries, walnuts, almonds, or pistachio nuts or other fillings

Preheat an oven to 375°F. In a bowl, beat the butter and sugar until light and fluffy. Beat in the egg, vanilla, lime zest, flour, and salt. Shape into a ball, cover, and refrigerate for 1 hour.

Break off walnut-sized pieces and roll them into 1-inch balls. Roll the balls in the ground nuts. Place on a baking sheet and push down on each ball with your thumb to make an indentation. Fill the indentation with a dab of jam, a chocolate chip, a bit of candied cherry, or a nut half or piece.

Bake for about 8 minutes, or until barely beginning to turn golden in color. Remove to a rack to cool. To store, pack in single layers, separated by waxed paper, in an airtight container. The cookies will keep for about 1 week. *Makes about 40 cookies*

Sugared Walnuts

MAKING THESE CRYSTAL-COATED NUTS IS A FUN AND EASY ACTIVITY FOR CHILDREN.

THEY WILL ENJOY PAINTING ON THE EGG WHITE WITH A BRUSH AND DIPPING THE WALNUT HALVES IN SUGAR.

THESE MAKE NICE HOMEMADE GIFTS FOR CHILDREN TO GIVE AS WELL AS TO EAT.

1/3 cup granulated sugar

1 teaspoon ground ginger

6 egg whites

3 cups (12 ounces) walnut halves

Preheat an oven to 325°F. In a bowl, combine the sugar and ginger and stir. In another bowl, lightly whisk or beat the egg whites just until frothy. Using a small paintbrush, lightly paint each walnut half with a small amount of the egg white, then sprinkle with the sugar mixture and place on an ungreased baking sheet.

When all the walnuts are coated, place the baking sheet in the oven until the nuts are toasted and crunchy and the coating is crisp, 15 to 20 minutes. Remove from the oven and let the nuts cool completely. Place them in an airtight container in single layers, separated by waxed paper. The nuts will keep for up to 3 months. *Makes 3 cups nuts*

Lollipops

LOLLIPOPS, EVEN FOR THE MOST NOVICE CANDY MAKER, ARE VERY SIMPLE TO MAKE. AS A PRECAUTION,
ADULTS SHOULD HANDLE THE MELTED SUGAR BECAUSE IT IS VERY HOT. CHILDREN, HOWEVER, CAN ARRANGE THE LOLLIPOP
STICKS, DIRECT THE COLOR AND FLAVORING CHOICES, AND LIFT THE COOLED LOLLIPOPS FROM THE BAKING SHEET.
LOLLIPOP STICKS CAN BE PURCHASED AT CRAFT STORES OR FROM CANDY-MAKING SUPPLY SHOPS.

5 tablespoons butter

1/2 cup light corn syrup

3/4 cup granulated sugar

1/2 teaspoon ground cinnamon or 1 teaspoon
cherry or mint extract

6 to 8 drops red or green food coloring, or as desired

Using 1 tablespoon of the butter, grease a large baking sheet. Arrange 18 lollipop sticks on the sheet, allowing at least 2-1/2 inches between each stick.

In a large saucepan, combine the remaining 4 tablespoons butter, corn syrup, and sugar. Cook over medium heat, stirring often, until the sugar dissolves. Insert a candy thermometer in the mixture and cook, stirring, until the thermometer reads 270°F. Remove from heat and stir in the flavoring and coloring. Let cool

for about 1 minute, or just until the syrup is easily pourable, but slightly thickened and able to hold its shape once poured.

Drop 1 tablespoon syrup onto the end of each stick, alternating ends.

Let cool thoroughly before lifting, about 10 minutes. To store, wrap each lollipop individually in clear cellophane wrap and tie with a ribbon. Pack in an airtight tin, where they will keep for up to 3 weeks. *Makes 18 lollipops*

tabletop sweets

7

Candy Wreath Napkin Rings

NAPKIN RINGS ADD A FINISHED NOTE TO TABLE SETTINGS,

AND IT IS FUN TO MAKE YOUR OWN TO REFLECT THE SEASON'S SPIRIT.

YOU WILL NEED:

12-inch lengths of decorative ribbon

Peppermint candy rings

Small jingle bells

TO MAKE:

Tie ribbon around the tops of candy rings where the candy ends meet. Thread jingle bells through ribbon ends before tying into a decorative bow. Place a napkin through each ring for each guest at the table.

Christmas-Cookie Napkin Rings

CHRISTMAS COOKIES MAKE VERSATILE NAPKIN RINGS BECAUSE YOU CAN EASILY VARY
THE SHAPES AND COLORS ACCORDING TO YOUR TABLE ACCESSORIES. IF DESIRED, CUSTOMIZE THEM
WITH THE GUEST'S NAME OR INITIALS WRITTEN IN ICING, OR USE NAME TAG CARDS.

YOU WILL NEED:

Frosted Ornament Cookies (page 49)

Small name-tag cards

Pen

12-inch lengths of decorative ribbon or cord

Napkins

TO MAKE:

Make the frosted ornament cookies with a small hole in the top of
each. Write the guests' names on the name tags. Thread each
cookie and name-tag card with ribbon or cord. Carefully wrap the
ribbon ends around each napkin and tie the ribbon in a bow or
decorative knot. Set a napkin ring at each place setting.

Juliet

Cookie Tree Centerpiece

A SMALL CHRISTMAS-COOKIE TREE HUNG WITH HOMEMADE ORNAMENT COOKIES MAKES
A LOVELY TABLE CENTERPIECE FOR THE HOME AND FOR HOLIDAY GATHERINGS. LET GUESTS AND CHILDREN
TAKE THE COOKIES HOME AS A DELICIOUS MEMENTO OF A FESTIVE OCCASION.

YOU WILL NEED:

Floral foam blocks

Bucket liner

Metal bucket or large ceramic container

Small handsaw

Small tabletop tree

Small Christmas tree lights or clip-on candles

Silver ornament balls and hooks

Frosted Ornament Cookies (page 49)

Decorative ribbon, cord, or string

TO MAKE:

Soak the floral foam in water. Add the liner to the bucket, if using, and fill the bucket or container with the foam and additional water.

Using the saw, cut the tree to the desired height. Insert the tree trunk in the foam and straighten it.

String the tree with lights or attach clip-on candles free of overhanging branches. Hang ornament balls on branches.

String the cookies carefully with ribbon and tie the ribbons to the branches.

Candy Stick Tree Centerpieces

THESE SMALL CANDY TREES MAKE IDEAL CENTERPIECES FOR CHILDREN'S PARTIES
AT SCHOOL OR AT HOME. MIXED WITH VOTIVE CANDLES, SMALL POTTED CYPRESS TREES, OR IVY TOPIARIES
THEY MAKE A MORE ELEGANT BUT FUN CENTERPIECE FOR A HOLIDAY ADULT OCCASION.

YOU WILL NEED:

Floral foam block

Decorative flowerpot or ceramic container

Sharp knife

3 to 4 dozen candy sticks

Hot-glue gun and glue sticks

Colored sugar

TO MAKE:

Fit the floral foam tightly into the pot or container, carving the
sides to fit with the knife. Carve the foam above the rim into a
cone shape.

Set aside one-third of the candy sticks. Break off one-third
of each of the remaining sticks. Starting with the unbroken sticks,
put a dab of glue on one end of each stick and, circling the cone
from the bottom up, insert the sticks as closely as possible about
1/2 inch into the foam. Continue, using shorter and shorter
sticks, until the cone is covered.

Dab hot glue in any gaps and sprinkle colored sugar into the
gaps to cover any exposed floral foam.

Chocolate Candy Tree Centerpieces

FOIL-WRAPPED CANDIES COME IN A VARIETY OF
BEAUTIFUL COVERINGS. THE ONES SHOWN HERE ARE FROM
GERMANY AND HAVE COLORFUL PAPER WINGS. YOU
CAN MAKE YOUR OWN WINGS WITH COLORED PAPERS AND
GLUE THEM TO CANDY WRAPPERS.

YOU WILL NEED:

Clear adhesive tape

Thin cord or ribbon

Foil-wrapped chocolate candies

Tabletop wire tree (available at crafts and
many housewares stores)

Small Christmas ornaments and hooks

Glue stick

TO MAKE:

With the adhesive tape, attach a loop of cord or ribbon to the
backs of half the candies. Using the glue stick, glue the papered
backs of matching candies together. Hang on the tree with other
ornaments, if desired.

pies, ices & creams

Double-Pecan Tart

PECANS ARE USED BOTH IN THE CRUST AND IN THE FILLING, GIVING THIS TART A RICH, THOROUGHLY
PECAN FLAVOR, WHICH IS HEIGHTENED BY ADDING A LITTLE COINTREAU OR OTHER ORANGE LIQUEUR. IF YOU
SERVE THIS WITH WHIPPED CREAM, ALSO FLAVOR IT WITH A LITTLE OF THE LIQUEUR.

CRUST

1 cup all-purpose flour

1/2 cup finely ground pecans

1/4 cup granulated sugar

1/2 cup (1 stick) butter, softened

1 egg

FILLING

2-1/2 cups coarsely chopped pecans

2 tablespoons butter, melted

1/2 cup firmly packed light brown sugar

2 eggs

1/4 cup Cointreau or other orange liqueur

1 teaspoon vanilla extract

To make the crust: Preheat an oven to 400°F. In a bowl, combine the flour, ground pecans, and sugar and stir until well blended. Add the butter and rub it into the dry ingredients with your fingertips until the mixture becomes crumblike. Add the egg, and using a fork, mix it into the dough. Using your hands, press the dough evenly into an 11-inch tart pan with a removable rim. Set aside.

To make the filling: Place the chopped pecans in a single layer on a baking sheet and toast for 5 to 6 minutes, turning once, until they are pale golden inside. Do not overtoast, as this will cause a slightly bitter flavor. Remove the pecans and set aside.

Lower the oven temperature to 350°F. In a large bowl, combine the melted butter, brown sugar, eggs, liqueur, and vanilla and mix until well blended. Stir in the toasted nuts. Pour the filling into the tart pan.

Bake in the lower third of the oven until the crust and filling are golden brown and the center has just barely set, 45 to 50 minutes. A toothpick inserted into the middle should come out slightly sticky. Overcooking will result in a curdled pie.

Transfer to a wire rack to cool for at least 1 hour. Serve warm or at room temperature. To serve, remove the pan rim and cut the pie into wedges. *Makes one 11-inch tart; serves 12*

Fold-Up Apple Tart with Dried Cranberries and Raisins

THIS EASY-TO-PREPARE RUSTIC TART IS MADE WITH FROZEN PUFF PASTRY, WHICH MEANS THE WHOLE TART CAN BE ASSEMBLED IN JUST A FEW MINUTES. THE RESULT—SWEET APPLES, STUDDED WITH CRANBERRIES AND SUCCULENT RAISINS AND BAKED IN A SWEET SYRUP—IS DECIDEDLY IMPRESSIVE. IF DESIRED, SERVE WITH VANILLA ICE CREAM.

2-1/2 to 3 pounds Golden Delicious or other sweet apples, cored, peeled, and sliced 1/4 inch thick

1/4 cup dried cranberries

1/4 cup raisins

1/3 cup granulated sugar

2 tablespoons all-purpose flour

2 tablespoons fresh lemon juice

1 sheet 10-by-16-inch frozen puff pastry, thawed

1-1/2 tablespoons unsalted butter, cut into small bits

Preheat an oven to 375°F. In a large bowl, combine the apples, cranberries, raisins, sugar, and flour and toss to coat well. Add the lemon juice and stir.

On a floured surface, roll out the pastry to make a 14-inch square. Trim off the corners to make a circle. Transfer the pastry to an ungreased baking sheet and spoon the fruit into the center, leaving about 2 inches of pastry uncovered around the edges. The fruit will be stacked high, but it will reduce as it cooks. Fold the rim of the pastry up over the fruit, pinching and tucking the dough as necessary. Dot the top of the fruit with the butter.

Bake for 30 minutes, or until the pastry is puffed and golden brown. Do not undercook.

Let stand for 10 to 15 minutes, loosely covered, before serving. Serve warm or at room temperature, cut into wedges. *Makes one 12-inch tart; serves 6 to 8*

Pear and Chocolate Tart

PEARS AND CHOCOLATE WERE MEANT FOR EACH OTHER, AND IN THIS VERSION OF A CLASSIC FRENCH TART, THE PEARS ARE
FIRST GLAZED WITH RASPBERRY PRESERVES, THEN DRIZZLED WITH CHOCOLATE THREADS.

PASTRY

1-3/4 cups all-purpose flour

1/4 cup sugar

1/2 cup (1 stick) cold unsalted butter, cut into pieces

1/4 teaspoon salt

1 egg, beaten with 2 tablespoons half-and-half

FILLING

4 pounds ripe, crisp pears such as Bosc or Bartlett

1 teaspoon fresh lemon juice

2 tablespoons plus 2/3 cup granulated sugar

1 tablespoon raspberry jam, sieved to remove seeds

1 tablespoon vanilla extract

3 tablespoons butter

1 tablespoon cornstarch, mixed with
1 tablespoon cold water

RASPBERRY GLAZE

1/2 cup raspberry jam, sieved to remove seeds

1 tablespoon granulated sugar

1 teaspoon powdered pectin

2 ounces bittersweet chocolate, cut into small pieces

To make the pastry: In a food processor, combine the flour, sugar, butter, and salt. Process until it becomes crumblike. Turn the mixture into a bowl, and using a fork, beat in the egg mixture until the dough holds together. Flatten it into a round about 2 to 2-1/2 inches thick, wrap in plastic wrap, and refrigerate for 1 hour.

To make the pastry shell: Preheat an oven to 425°F. Place the dough on a sheet of waxed paper on a work surface. Sprinkle the dough with flour and place another sheet of waxed paper on top. Using a rolling pin, roll the dough out 1/4-inch thick to form a 12-inch circle. Remove the top sheet and transfer the dough to a 9-1/2 by 2-1/2-inch tart pan with a removable bottom. Trim the excess pastry so it is even with the rim of the pan. Line the pastry with aluminum foil and weight it with dried beans or pie weights. Bake for 10 minutes, then take out of the oven and remove the foil and weights. Reduce the oven temperature to 325°F, return the pan to the oven, and bake until the center of the shell is firm, 5 to 6 minutes. Transfer the pan to a wire rack to cool.

To make the filling: Peel and core the pears, then cut 1/4-inch-thick slices into a bowl. Put 3 cups of the pear slices into a shallow baking dish carefully, so as not to bruise or break them. Sprinkle with the lemon juice and the 2 tablespoons sugar and set aside.

In a large saucepan, cook the remaining pears over low heat until tender, stirring occasionally, 10 to 15 minutes. Add the raspberry jam, vanilla, the 2/3 cup sugar, and the butter. Increase heat to high and boil, stirring, until a thick sauce begins to form, about 10 minutes. Purée. Stir in the cornstarch mixture until the sauce has thickened to a very stiff texture resembling applesauce, 3 to 4 more minutes.

Pour the thickened pear sauce into the bottom of the pastry shell, spreading it evenly in a layer a scant 1/2-inch thick. Arrange the sliced pears in concentric rings on top, making an attractive pattern.

Bake for 20 to 25 minutes, or until the sliced pears are tender and lightly golden. Remove and set aside to cool to room temperature, about 1 hour.

To make the raspberry glaze: In a saucepan, combine the sieved raspberries, sugar, and pectin over medium heat and bring to a boil, stirring to dissolve the sugar and the pectin. Cook until thick enough to coat the back of a metal spoon and leave a path when you draw a spoon through it, about 225°F on a candy thermometer. Spoon the warm glaze over the pears to make a thin coating.

In the top of a double boiler over barely simmering water, melt the chocolate, stirring. Using a spoon, drizzle the chocolate in thin threads over the surface of the glazed pears. Let cool until the chocolate threads have set, about 20 minutes. Refrigerate until the glaze is firm, 2 to 3 hours. Serve chilled. *Serves 8*

Apple-Quince Pie

QUINCE, AN OLD-FASHIONED FRUIT WITH A FIRM FLESH AND A BIT OF CITRUS TASTE, COMBINES WITH APPLES AND RAISINS TO MAKE A FALL HOLIDAY PIE THAT CAN BE SERVED WARM ON ITS OWN OR WITH ICE CREAM.

CRUST

2 cups all-purpose flour

1 teaspoon salt

3/4 cup (1-1/2 sticks) butter

2 teaspoons distilled white or cider vinegar

2 tablespoons granulated sugar

1/2 cup ice water

FILLING

2-1/2 pounds tart apples such as Granny Smith, peeled, cored, and cut into 1/4-inch-thick slices

2 quinces, peeled, cored, and cut into 1/4-inch-thick slices

1/2 cup raisins

1 teaspoon finely grated lemon zest

1 tablespoon fresh lemon juice

1/4 cup firmly packed dark brown sugar

1/4 cup granulated sugar

1/4 cup all-purpose flour

1/4 teaspoon freshly ground cloves

1/4 teaspoon freshly grated nutmeg

3 tablespoons softened butter, cut into small bits

To make the crust: In a food processor, combine the flour, salt, and butter, and process just until the mixture has a coarse, grainy texture. Add the vinegar and sugar and process to blend. Add the ice water and process just until a rough ball begins to form. Remove, wrap in plastic wrap and refrigerate for 4 hours. Unwrap and let stand at room temperature for about 20 minutes to become pliable. Preheat an oven to 350°F.

On a floured work surface, divide the dough into 2 pieces, one slightly larger than the other. Roll the larger piece into a circle 1/4-inch thick and about 12 inches in diameter. Loosely drape the circle over the rolling pin and transfer to a 9-inch pie pan. Press the dough into the pan, leaving at least a 1/2-inch overhang. Refrigerate while making the filling.

To make the filling: In a large bowl, combine the apples, quinces, raisins, lemon zest, and juice. Sprinkle with the sugars, flour, cloves, and nutmeg; stir to mix well. Spoon the filling into the chilled pie crust, heaping it higher in the center. Scatter bits of butter over top.

Roll the remaining dough out into an 11-inch circle. Drape the circle over the rolling pin and place it on top of the pie. Tuck the edges of the upper crust under those of the lower, pinching them together to seal them. Make three or four 1-inch slashes in the upper crust to allow steam to escape.

Bake for 40 to 45 minutes, or until the crust is golden brown. Serve warm or at room temperature, cut into wedges. *Makes one 9-inch pie; serves 6*

Hazelnut Ice Cream with Dried Cherry and Raspberry Sauce

HAZELNUTS, ALSO CALLED FILBERTS, HAVE A FIRM, CRUNCHY TEXTURE AND A WONDERFUL NUTTY FLAVOR. THE SAUCE, A DEEP GARNET RED, SWEET AND FRESH, IS A DELICIOUS COMPANION TO THE ICE CREAM.

1 cup (5 ounces) hazelnuts, toasted and skinned

2 cups heavy cream

2 cups milk

1/2 cup firmly packed light brown sugar

1/4 cup granulated sugar

1/4 teaspoon salt

4 egg yolks

SAUCE

1/2 cup dried cherries

1/2 cup water

2 teaspoons granulated sugar

1 cup red raspberries

Coarsely chop all but 1/4 cup of the nuts and set aside.

In a large, heavy saucepan, combine the cream, milk, sugars, and salt. Bring to a boil over medium-high heat, stirring often, until the sugar has dissolved. In a large bowl, whisk the yolks until they change to a lemon color. Gradually whisk about 1 cup of the hot milk mixture into the yolks. Now, whisk the yolk mixture into the hot milk mixture and continue to cook, stirring constantly, until the mixture thickens enough to coat the back of a metal spoon. Chill the mixture for 2 to 3 hours. Freeze in an ice cream maker according to the manufacturer's directions. When the ice cream has thickened and firmed slightly, stir in the chopped nuts and continue freezing.

To make the sauce: In a saucepan, combine the dried cherries, water, and sugar. Bring to a boil over medium-high heat and cook for 3 to 4 minutes, or until the cherries are slightly softened. Reduce heat to low and continue to cook, simmering, for about 10 minutes, or until the cherries are quite soft. Add the raspberries and cook another 2 minutes. Purée in a food mill or a blender, then strain.

To serve, pour a little sauce on the bottom of each dessert plate. Add a scoop or two of ice cream and sprinkle with a few of the reserved whole hazelnuts. *Makes about 1 quart ice cream and 1 cup sauce*

Toasting and Skinning Hazelnuts

Preheat an oven to 400°F. On a baking sheet, spread the hazelnuts in a single layer and toast for 6 to 7 minutes, or until they are light-golden inside. Do not overtoast, or they will have a slightly bitter flavor. Place the nuts in a kitchen towel and rub them together to remove as much of the papery outer coating as possible.

Sugared Fruit Topping for Ice Cream

DIPPED IN EGG WHITES AND THEN ROLLED IN SUGAR, FRUITS BECOME CRYSTALLIZED, SPARKLING ORNAMENT TOPPINGS FOR ICE CREAM. SMALLER FRUITS, SUCH AS GRAPES, KUMQUATS, AND CHERRIES ARE GOOD CHOICES, AND ALL GO WELL WITH CHOCOLATE OR VANILLA ICE CREAM.

3 egg whites

1 cup superfine sugar

1 cup stemmed grapes, kumquats, or other small fruit

Put the egg whites in a large bowl and whisk until frothy but not stiff. Pour the sugar in a small bowl.

Place the fruit in a single, well-spaced layer on a sheet of waxed paper.

Using a small paintbrush, brush each piece of fruit with egg white, then put it in the sugar bowl and spoon the sugar over it. Using tweezers or small tongs, carefully lift up the fruit piece and shake off any excess sugar. Transfer each piece to the waxed paper to dry.

Repeat until all the fruit has been sugared. If the egg whites lose their frothiness, whisk them again.

Let the fruit stand overnight in a dry location or until ready to use the next day. The toppings should be used within 24 hours of sugaring. *Makes about 1 cup*

Peppermint Ice Cream

CHILDREN—AND ADULTS TOO—ARE FANS OF PEPPERMINT
ICE CREAM. COLORED PALEST PINK AND DOTTED WITH BITS OF
PEPPERMINT, THE SCOOPS CAN BE SERVED IN CONES OR BOWLS.
THIS IS ESPECIALLY GOOD WITH CHOCOLATE CAKE.

2 cups heavy cream

2 cups milk

3/4 cup granulated sugar

1/4 teaspoon salt

4 egg yolks

1 teaspoon peppermint extract

4 ounces hard peppermint candies,
crushed into small pieces

In a large, heavy saucepan, combine the cream, milk, sugar, and salt. Bring to a boil over medium-high heat and cook, stirring often, until the sugar has dissolved.

In a bowl, whisk the yolks together until they change to a lemon color. Gradually whisk about 1 cup of the hot milk mixture into the yolks. Now, whisk the yolk mixture into the hot milk mixture and continue to cook, stirring constantly, until the mixture thickens enough to coat the back of a metal spoon. Refrigerate for 2 to 3 hours. Add the peppermint extract, stirring well. Freeze in an ice cream maker according to the manufacturer's instructions. When the ice cream is partially frozen, stir in the candies. *Makes about 1 quart*

Chocolate-Peppermint Mousse

CHOCOLATE MOUSSE, SO THICK AND INTENSELY CHOCOLATE,
IS ALWAYS A WELCOME DESSERT. FLAVORING IT WITH A LITTLE
PEPPERMINT GIVES IT A SURPRISE HOLIDAY TWIST.

4 ounces bittersweet chocolate, finely chopped

3 tablespoons butter, softened and cut into small pieces

3 eggs

1/2 teaspoon peppermint extract

1/4 teaspoon salt

1/4 cup confectioners' sugar

Melt the chocolate in the top of a double boiler over barely simmering water. Add the butter and cook, stirring, until the butter has melted and is incorporated into the chocolate.

Separate 1 egg, putting the white in a large bowl and the yolk into the chocolate. Whisk the yolk into the chocolate, fully incorporating it. Repeat this process with the remaining 2 eggs. Stir the peppermint extract into the chocolate mixture.

Remove the chocolate mixture from heat and let cool to lukewarm. Add the salt to the egg whites, and using an electric mixer, beat them on medium-high until they form stiff, glossy peaks. Beat in the confectioners' sugar.

Fold the egg whites into the chocolate, being careful not to deflate the egg whites. Spoon the mousse into a bowl or individual serving bowls and refrigerate for at least 6 hours before serving, or until the mousse is very firm. *Serves 4*

Eggnog Ice Cream Profiteroles

PROFITEROLES, THE FRENCH DESSERT OF CREAM PUFFS FILLED WITH ICE CREAM OR PASTRY CREAM, LOOK VERY FANCY BUT ARE ACTUALLY QUITE EASY TO MAKE. IF YOU WISH TO TAKE A SHORTCUT, USE STORE-BOUGHT ICE CREAM. A TRAY OF THESE PRESENTED AT DINNER'S END WILL DRAW RAVE REVIEWS FOR BOTH PRESENTATION AND FLAVOR.

ICE CREAM

2 cups eggnog

2 cups milk

3/4 cup granulated sugar

1/4 teaspoon salt

4 egg yolks

1/4 teaspoon ground nutmeg

1/4 teaspoon ground mace

1/4 teaspoon ground ginger

CREAM PUFFS

1 cup water

6-1/2 tablespoons unsalted butter

1/2 teaspoon salt

1-1/4 cups all-purpose flour

4 eggs, plus 1 egg beaten with 1 teaspoon water

CHOCOLATE GLAZE

2 cups confectioners' sugar

1/4 cup unsweetened cocoa powder

3 to 4 tablespoons milk

To make the ice cream: In a heavy saucepan, combine the eggnog, milk, sugar, and salt. Bring to a boil over medium-high heat and cook, stirring often, until the sugar has dissolved. In a large bowl, whisk the yolks together until they change to a lemon color. Gradually whisk about 1 cup of the hot milk mixture into the yolks. Now, whisk the yolk mixture into the hot milk mixture and continue to cook, stirring constantly, until the mixture thickens enough to coat the back of a metal spoon. Add the nutmeg, mace, and ginger, stirring well. Refrigerate the mixture for 2 to 3 hours. Freeze in an ice cream maker according to the manufacturer's instructions.

To make the cream puffs: Preheat an oven to 425°F. In a heavy saucepan, combine the water, 6 tablespoons of the butter, and the salt over medium-high heat and bring to a boil. Cook until the butter melts, then remove from heat and add the flour all at once, beating with a wooden spoon until incorporated. Return to the heat and continue to beat vigorously until the mixture pulls away from the sides of the pan and holds together, about 2 minutes.

Remove the saucepan from the heat. Make a well in the center of the mixture and break one of the 4 eggs into it. Beat to incorporate the egg. Repeat until all 4 eggs have been added and the mixture has become a smooth paste.

Using the remaining 1/2 tablespoon butter, grease a baking sheet. Fill a cup with hot water. Dip a large metal spoon first into the hot water and then into the paste. Using your finger or another spoon, push heaping tablespoons of the paste off the spoon and onto the baking sheet. Repeat, spacing the puffs about 2 inches apart. Dip the spoon into hot water and gently press it onto each puff to smooth the surface.

Using a pastry brush, coat just the top surface of the puff with the egg-water mixture. Do not allow the egg mixture to dribble down the sides, or it will bind the paste puff to the baking sheet and prevent puffing.

Bake until the puffs are golden brown and have increased in size by about 1-1/2 times, 20 to 25 minutes. Remove from the oven and pierce each puff with a skewer to release the steam. Let cool for 10 to 15 minutes before slitting. Slit through the middle to make a top and a bottom.

To make the chocolate glaze: Sift the confectioners' sugar and the cocoa powder together into a medium bowl. Add 3 tablespoons of the milk and mix. It will be quite stiff. If too stiff to spread, add up to 1 tablespoon milk, a few drops at a time, until stiff but spreadable. Spread each profiterole top with a little of the chocolate icing. It will soften and spread on the warm surface. Set aside.

To serve, place the profiterole bottoms on a platter. Place a large tablespoon-sized scoop of ice cream in each and top with an iced top. Serve immediately. *Makes about 30 medium puffs; serves 15*

Lemon Verbena Crème Brûlée

A BEGUILING HINT OF FRAGRANT LEMON VERBENA FLAVORS THESE RICH CUSTARDS, WITH THEIR CRACKED TOPS OF HARDENED SUGAR. A CRÈME BRÛLÉE IRON OR KITCHEN BLOWTORCH CAN BE USED TO MELT THE SUGAR FOR A SMOOTH, PROFESSIONAL APPEARANCE. IF MELTED UNDER THE BROILER INSTEAD, THE CUSTARDS MAY LOOK A LITTLE MORE RUSTIC, BUT THEY WILL TASTE JUST AS GOOD. YOU CAN EXPERIMENT WITH OTHER FLAVORINGS TOO, SUCH AS DRIED LAVENDER BLOSSOMS.

2 cups heavy cream

1/4 cup granulated sugar

12 fresh lemon verbena leaves

4 egg yolks

1/2 teaspoon vanilla extract

4 tablespoons firmly packed brown sugar

Preheat an oven to 325°F. In a medium saucepan, combine the cream and sugar. Cook over medium-high heat, stirring, just until tiny bubbles form around the edge and the sugar has dissolved, 3 to 4 minutes. Remove from heat, add the lemon verbena leaves, and let stand for 15 minutes.

In a bowl, beat the egg yolks with the vanilla extract just until thickened. Reheat the cream mixture to just below a simmer, then whisk it into the egg yolks. Strain the mixture through a fine-meshed sieve, discarding the leaves and any threads of cooked egg.

Pour the mixture into four 6-ounce ramekins, filling each to within a scant 1/2 inch of the top. Place the ramekins in a baking dish, pour hot water around them to reach halfway up the sides, and bake for about 50 minutes, or until a thin skin has formed on the tops and the custards are just barely set; the center should slightly quiver. To test for doneness, slip a knife two-thirds of the way down the side. The knife should come out clean or with just the tiniest stickiness. As the custard cools, it will continue to cook and become firmer.

Remove and let cool to room temperature, then refrigerate for at least 3 to 4 hours.

To finish, preheat a broiler. Sprinkle the top of each custard evenly with 1 tablespoon of brown sugar by pushing it through a small sieve with the back of a teaspoon. Place the ramekins in a baking dish, pour cold water around them, and add several ice cubes. Place about 3 inches from the broiler and broil just until the sugar melts, 2 to 3 minutes.

Remove and let cool until the surface hardens, at least 10 minutes. They can be refrigerated for several hours before serving. *Serves 4*

Metric Conversion Table

LIQUID WEIGHTS

U.S. Measurements	Metric Equivalents
1/4 teaspoon	1.23 ml
1/2 teaspoon	2.5 ml
3/4 teaspoon	3.7 ml
1 teaspoon	5 ml
1 dessertspoon	10 ml
1 tablespoon (3 teaspoons)	15 ml
2 tablespoons (1 ounce)	30 ml
1/4 cup	60 ml
1/3 cup	80 ml
1/2 cup	120 ml
2/3 cup	160 ml
3/4 cup	180 ml
1 cup (8 ounces)	240 ml
2 cups (1 pint)	480 ml
3 cups	720 ml
4 cups (1 quart)	1 liter
4 quarts (1 gallon)	3.8 liters

DRY WEIGHTS

U.S. Measurements	Metric Equivalents
1/4 ounce	7 grams
1/3 ounce	10 grams
1/2 ounce	14 grams
1 ounce	28 grams
1-1/2 ounces	42 grams
1-3/4 ounces	50 grams
2 ounces	57 grams
3-1/2 ounces	100 grams
4 ounces (1/4 pound)	114 grams
6 ounces	170 grams
8 ounces (1/2 pound)	227 grams
9 ounces	250 grams
16 ounces (1 pound)	464 grams

TEMPERATURES

Fahrenheit	Celsius (Centigrade)
32°F (water freezes)	0°C
200°F	95°C
212°F (water boils)	100°C
250°F	120°C
275°F	135°C
300°F (slow oven)	150°C
325°F	160°C
350°F (moderate oven)	175°C
375°F	190°C
400°F (hot oven)	205°C
425°F	220°C
450°F (very hot oven)	230°C
475°F	245°C
500°F (extremely hot oven)	260°C

LENGTH

U.S. Measurements	Metric Equivalents
1/8 inch	3 mm
1/4 inch	6 mm
3/8 inch	1 cm
1/2 inch	1.2 cm
3/4 inch	2 cm
1 inch	2.5 cm
1-1/4 inches	3.1 cm
1-1/2 inches	3.7 cm
2 inches	5 cm
3 inches	7.5 cm
4 inches	10 cm

APPROXIMATE EQUIVALENTS

1 kilo is slightly more than 2 pounds.

1 liter is slightly more than 1 quart.

1 centimeter is approximately 3/8 inch.

Index